Edwin A. Perry

Modern observations on rifle shooting,

with an improved system of score book, and including silicate slate for use on the range

Edwin A. Perry

Modern observations on rifle shooting,
with an improved system of score book, and including silicate slate for use on the range

ISBN/EAN: 9783337712334

Printed in Europe, USA, Canada, Australia, Japan

Cover: Foto ©Andreas Hilbeck / pixelio.de

More available books at **www.hansebooks.com**

THIRD EDITION.

Modern Observations

—ON—

RIFLE SHOOTING,

—WITH AN—

IMPROVED SYSTEM OF SCORE BOOK,

—AND INCLUDING—

SILICATE SLATE FOR USE ON THE RANGE.

(Printed on Green Paper to shield the eyes from bright sunlight.)

Price Entire, - - - - **$1.00.**

EDWIN A. PERRY,

AUTHOR.

E. REMINGTON & SONS, Publishers,

281 & 283 Broadway, N. Y. City.

Copyrighted. 1880. by EDWIN A. PERRY.

PREFACE.

In presenting the within conclusions, drawn entirely from original personal observations and practice, the writer has endeavored to savor them with a concise conversational manner of presentment.

However unimportant little things may appear, none are overlooked here.

What has proved so perplexing with all other works on Rifle Shooting is herein avoided; each item having a separate heading, properly indexed, thus enabling the riflemen to turn instantly to the information desired.

The young rifleman will not necessarily be encouraged to enter the lists when he discovers that his pathway is beset with so many obstacles. It is *not* however the fact that satisfactory results cannot be obtained by beginners; and, once started, the infatuation with the science comes in the continued victories over these very obstacles. In all phases of rifle shooting it is a glorious fact that all of the difficulties treated on herein do not combine as an army to obstruct the path to the bull's-eye at one time, but, like the legions of the Army of the Potomac in its earlier history, they present themselves in detail for defeat at the hands of moderate skill.

The diffidence that the author might feel in treating so arbitrarily on the very many points on which the best riflemen honestly differ is overcome by the fact that no rules exist on competent authority to be overturned by the writer's treatment, and the conclusions are arrived at by the light that close attention and careful experiment can only give.

It would be natural to expect in a science resting on so many principles that the first attempt to bring all those principles into subjection would meet with criticism which would modify positions taken. Within the years that this book has been before the public, no writer of original matter or criticism has differed with the manual. The conclusion is that its rules are correct and deserving of careful study.

In changing the score diagrams, the field of usefulness of the book is enlarged. Sir Henry Halford very kindly gave the suggestion, and the short and mid-range shooters desired it. Care has been taken to preserve the identity of the 1st class target. The dotted circle in the long-range bull's eye will serve as a carton or for a mid-range bull's eye, and is all the alteration needed to complete a 2d class target, as the *outer circle* is obsolete here. The other dotted circles form a 3d class target. The spaces for writing in conditions have been materially enlarged, and this doubtless leaves the book without cause for objection.

The work has been supported not only by the men who needed it for constant use, but by the *advertisers*. The author saw that without their aid failure would be the result, with their aid a good article could be produced. Riflemen should therefore feel kindly toward the advertisers for helping them to buy a good score-book and slate.

The green paper has proved successful in shielding the eyes from the reflection of the bright sun, and has probably contributed to the favor in which the book is generally held.

An article on long-range, with military rifles, has been added.

In view of the fact that position and sights for Military Rifles have been revolutionized, the author respectfully calls attention to his caustic words on pages 15, 23 and 24, written on those subjects in advance of the changes made.

The author requested the representative exponents of the two styles of off-hand shooting, viz., off-hand and hip-rest, to write articles on, and furnish their pictures taken in, their favorite positions. This was done in a spirit of fairness to the devotees of both styles. Capt. W. H. Jackson has complied but * * * * declined, as he was "not necessarily tenacious about his position." The author understands that he is now practicing *off-hand proper*.

The article on the Long-range Tournament is, the author believes, the first attempt yet made to make a scientific tabulation and deduction from such a match, and as the tables and targets selected for elevation are published, the reader is enabled to follow or disagree with the author's treatment. Originating the match for the purpose, shooting in it with the preconceived idea of watching every detail, the author gladly accepts the responsibility of his conclusions.

At the request of a great many the old slate is restored, but the new diagrams are retained in the book out of deference to the Short and Mid-range shooters.

The writer respectfully calls attention to the fact that this book *is* NOT *gathered from obsolete authorities*. There are no effete notions in it. It is not voluble in verbiage, but is terse, original, modern and complete.

Very respectfully,

EDWIN A. PERRY.

Sharps Long Range Rifle, Model 1878.

Used by Bruce, Selph, Weber, Blydenburgh, Allen, Jewell, Gildersleeve, Sanford, Glynn, Hawley, Arms, Eyrich, Hyde, and by nearly every other first-class shot in the country.

Approximate Elevation for Sharps Long Range Rifles, with Vernier on grip.

200 Yards	11	800 103
300 "	23	900 121
400 "	38	1000 139
500 "	54	1100 160
600 "	70	1200 180
700 "	86	

With Vernier on heel, add about 25 per cent. to above.

Sharps Rifle, Model 1878.
Sectional View, Showing Action Closed.

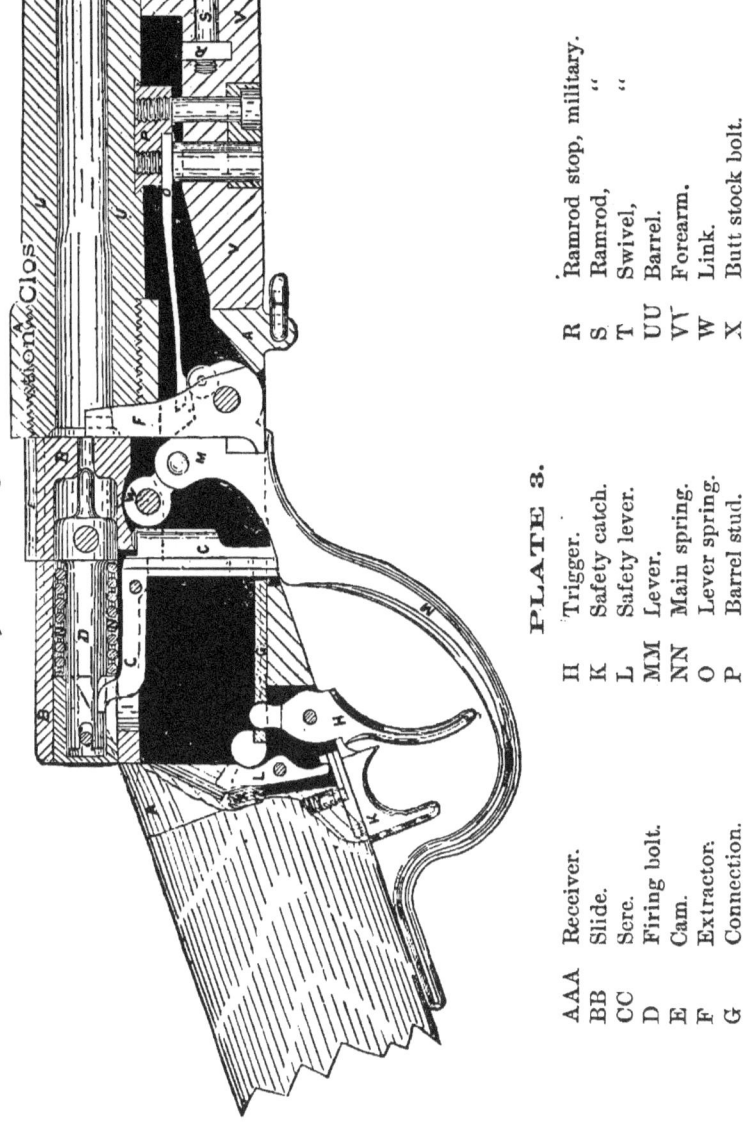

PLATE 3.

AAA	Receiver.	H	Trigger.
BB	Slide.	K	Safety catch.
CC	Scre.	L	Safety lever.
D	Firing bolt.	MM	Lever.
E	Cam.	NN	Main spring.
F	Extractor.	O	Lever spring.
G	Connection.	P	Barrel stud.

R	Ramrod stop, military.
S	Ramrod, "
T	Swivel, "
UU	Barrel.
VV	Forearm.
W	Link.
X	Butt stock bolt.

INDEX.

	PAGE.
Accident	20
Acids	17
Aiming	23, 25
Allowance for Elevation and Wind	32
Ammunition, Loading	20, 21
Anger	34, 36
Angle of Hit	33
Anvil	16
Association Regulations	45
Attention	34, 35
Ball Starter	18
" Seater	19
Barometer	30
Beginning Score	24
Beginner	13
Borrowing	35
Bullets	17, 19, 20, 36
Cap	16, 20, 36
Cap Extractor	18
Cartridges, Loading	20
Cautiousness	35
Chambering	14
Cleaning Rifle	21
" Shells	16
" Rods	21
Clothing	33
Clouds	26, 27
Coaching	35
Cold and Heat	29
Contesting Shots	34
Conversation	34
Diet	33
Delaying Target	35
Direction of Wind	29
Elevations	17, 26, 29, 30, 32, &c.
See headings that call for changes.	
Excitement	34, 36
Exercise	33
Experiment	34
Eye	26, 27
" Glasses	26
Figuring Elevations	32
Firing, Errors in pull off	25, 36
Fixed Ammunition	13, 20, 21
Fleeting Clouds	26, 27, 28, 36
Flinch	23
Force of Wind	29
Fog	26
Front Position	24
Funnel with Tube	19, 20
Generosity	35

	PAGE.
Getting Elevations	32
Glass Spotting	31
Goose Eggs	35
Heat and Cold	29
Holding Plumb	15, 24, 31
Hygrometer	30
Keeping Score	31, 35
Kneeling	23
Leading (ledding)	21
Light	28, 36
" and Shade	26, 27, 28, 36
Line of Sight	23
Loading Implements	18
" Rifle	20
" Ammunition	20
Locality at Firing Point	23
Long-range Outfit	13
Low Position	22
Markers	34, 36
Measures and Weights	19
Mid-range Position	23
" Outfit	13
Mind	34
Mirage	26
Moisture	30
Muzzle-Loader	14, 21
Nerves	23, 35
Oil	21
Offhand	23
Outfit for Beginner	13
" " Mid-range	13
" " Long-range	13
Packing Cartridges	20
Patches on Bullets	18
Personal Habits	33
Plumbing Sights	15, 16
Politeness	35
Powder	17, 19, 20, 36
Position	22, 23, 24, 36
Protesting	34
Prone Position	24
Preface	5
Pull-Off	23, 24, 25
Pulling the Trigger	25
Quarreling	34
Reasons for Failures	36
Recapper	18
Rifle, Care of	14
" Cleaning	21
" Failures on account of	36

Rifle, Kind 14	Table of Differences in Elevation, &c.	32
" Loading 20	Table of Weights and Measures .	19
" Muzzle-Loaders . . . 14	Talking	34
Rods for Cleaning 21	Target—Shooting on Wrong . .	35
Rules and Regulations Associations 45	Targets—Small with Pegs . .	31
Running for Train . . . 14, 33	Team Shooting 39, 40,	41
Scales and Weights 19	Telescope 26,	31
Score Diagrams 66	Thermometer	29
Shade and Light . . 26, 27, 28, 36	Time	36
Shades on the Sights . . . 16	Title	3
Shell Crimper 18	Trajectory	32
Shells 16, 20, 36	Tube with Funnel . . . 19,	20
Shoes 33	Unaccountable	36
Shooting on Wrong Target . . 35		
Sights 14, 36	Verdigris	16
" Discs 16	Vernier (see Elevations) . .	15
Sighting Shots 24	Wad 18,	21
" Errors in . . . 24, 28	" Rigby and Metford . . 18, 21,	22
Silicate Slate 5	Walking Fast	33
Snapping Shots . . . 23, 24, 25	Warming Shots 24,	25
Spectacles 26	Weather 25,	30
Spirit Level 15, 36	Weights and Measures . . .	19
Spotting Shots 31	Weighing Powder and Bullet .	20
Summary 32, 62, 63	Wind 28, 32,	36
Sunlight 26, 27, 28	Wrong Target, Shooting on . .	3

UNITED STATES CARTRIDGE COMPANY

LOWELL, MASS.

MANUFACTURERS OF THE

BRASS, SOLID HEAD, CENTRAL FIRE, RELOADING SHELLS AND CARTRIDGES.

Adapted to all Military and Sporting Rifles and Pistols, and in use by the

ARMY and NAVY of the UNITED STATES,

and several Foreign Governments. Rim-fire ammunition of all kinds. Special attention given to the manufacture of

Cartridges for Target Practice.

Send for Illustrated Catalogue.

FOWLER & FULTON, General Agents,   **300 Broadway, N. Y.**

MODEL OF 1876.

75 Grains of Powder, 350 Grain Bullet, Calibre, 45-100.

Especially adapted to Mid-Range Shooting, and to the Sportsman's use. Combining accuracy and rapidity as a *Single Loader* or *Repeater*. This Gun will be found to meet the only possible want of the Hunter or Sportsman as yet unfilled.

Manufacturers of every description of
MILITARY AND SPORTING METALLIC AMMUNITION.

WINCHESTER REPEATING RIFLE.
MODEL 1873.

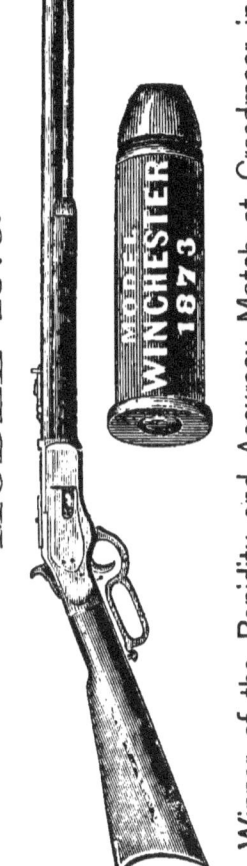

Winner of the Rapidity and Accuracy Match at Creedmoor in 1876.

FOR THE HUNTER, INDISPENSABLE.
For the SETTLER on the Indian Frontier, A NECESSITY.

It is Simple, Strong, Light, Handy, Accurate, and Unequaled for

RAPIDITY OF FIRE.

For any further information, address

Winchester Repeating Arms Co.
NEW HAVEN, CONN.

JAMES G. DIMOND'S IRON WORKS,
ESTABLISHED 1852.
Nos. 209 & 211 West Thirty-third Street, NEW YORK.
Manufacturers of Iron Store Fronts, Columns, Beams, Doors, Shutters, Skylights, Gratings, Railings, Vault and Area Lights, and Iron Work in General.

Also, Manufacturers of the American Cast Iron, Chilled Faced, Regulation
CREEDMOOR TARGETS,

Endorsed by all the best Judges in the Country who have seen or used them.

Size of Plates, 2 ft. x 6 ft. By placing two or more Plates together, you can form 1st, 2d and 3d Class Targets.

They have during the past season, been put to the most severe tests of Company and Platoon Firing, and have proved far superior to the imported English Targets. The Targets are made of a quality of iron specially adapted for the purpose.

Guaranteed against all Imperfections; thoroughly tested before delivery, in reference to Flaws, Sand, or Blow-holes.

The following are some of the Testimonials Received:

JAMES G. DIMOND, Esq.   New York, Jan. 2, 1878.
Dear Sir—It gives me pleasure to say, that the Iron Targets manufactured by you and used at Creedmoor during the past year, have given very general satisfaction as to durability and strength, they having been subjected to many severe tests by the different distances and classes of firing.   Very Respectfully,
     Capt. JOSEPH G. STORY, Member of Range Com. N.R.A.

JAMES G. DIMOND, Esq.   New York, Dec. 27, 1877.
Dear Sir—The Targets furnished by you for the Range at Creedmoor have stood the severest test during the season of 1877, and have given general satisfaction. I can cheerfully recommend them as being equal in all respects to those imported from England. Yours, etc.,
     Col. GEO. D. SCOTT, Member of Range Committee.

J. G. DIMOND, Esq.   New York, Jan. 4, 1878.
Dear Sir—In reply to your letter of 11th inst., I would state, that the first Targets furnished by you were a little rough on the edges, but have stood the test which has been applied to them. The last have been all right. Respectfully yours,
     Col. GEO. W. WINGATE, Chairman of Range Com. N. R. A. of A.

MR. J. G. DIMOND: Creedmoor, Jan. 19, 1878.
Dear Sir—The Target Slabs furnished by you, and now in use, are far superior to any ever used here. Yours truly,   WM. H. BROWER, Supt. of Range.

JAMES G. DIMOND, Esq.   New York, Jan. 5, 1878.
Dear Sir—By close observation of the effect of the Rifle practice at the Creedmoor Range during the past season, upon the Targets of the National Rifle Association, I am convinced that the Target Plates furnished by you met every reasonable requirement, and are in all respects superior to the imported Iron Target.
     Genl. DANIEL D. WYLIE, Chief of Ordnance, S. N. Y.

MODERN OBSERVATIONS ON RIFLE SHOOTING.

OUTFIT FOR A BEGINNER.

A beginner should always start at short-range where he can acquire quick results, the elements offering but little opposition. Here steadiness and the art of holding a rifle properly can be acquired, and deviations, scarcely ever great enough to take the bullet off the target, can readily be discovered by the unassisted eye. Any military rifle, some india-rubber and matches to blacken the sights, a wooden rod and flannel patches for occasional cleaning, the requisite quantity of fixed ammunition and a score book, are quite enough to establish the quality of the man.

OUTFIT FOR MID-RANGE.

Satisfied to know more of the art, sporting rifles should next be employed; they involve cleaning after each shot. Three wiping rods, one for brush; a bottle of water, and a little sperm oil should be added. A good glass for spotting the hits is necessary, and a neat box for carrying the apparatus will be found very handy. A general remark as to the elements is sufficient, and ammunition, to be had ready made, is yet quite good enough. Here at mid-range, the eye becomes accustomed to the fine sights and the position becomes confirmed. Fine shooting is often the result at this range.

OUTFIT FOR LONG-RANGE.

A fine breech-loading rifle, the best made, having pistol grip, a full sett of fine sights, Vernier, wind-guage, spirit-level, and extra front sight discs; loading implements, viz., recapper and cap seater, ball starter ball seater, shell crimper, funnel with tube, and scales and weights; barometer, thermometer, hygrometer, long-range glass and stand; ammunition and implement case, a fine score book, one wooden rod with brush, three wooden rods with slit, water bottle, oil and can and brass shells, powder, bullets and caps *ad libitum.*

RIFLES.

It is not the author's intention to attempt a treatise on rifles, beginning with the one used on the ark. A few homely suggestions, as to generalities, will not interfere with the rifle makers altitudinous dome of thought, and may prove sign posts to guide young riflemen. If muzzle-loaders could be cleaned after each shot, with the same ease and certainty as breech loaders, they would prove much the best shooters, as they can stand lightning powder and hard bullets; and consequently very light rifling; as it is, without cleaning, they have, in the hands of the foreign teams, proved worthy of the highest consideration for accuracy; while there is little trouble in loading, none in cleaning, and no shells to cart around and pay for.

It is conceded, however, that the breech-loaders, made for rapid shooting, prove the best for fine work; as the rifleman is able to shoot from an absolutely clean barrel each time. Labor in cleaning, time in loading, expense and all other inconveniences, are as nothing in comparison with one more point on a good score. In a breech-loader look for a good, thick barrel with a pronounced but light rifling, minus all attempts at gaining twist; a fine breech action not liable to accident or to be sprung by the powder, chambered for a short shell, pistol grip and fine sights. All of the foregoing refers to fine long-range or mid-range rifles. For short-range a breech-loader that does not require cleaning more than once in ten shots, of almost any make, is good enough.

In the advertising pages each rifle of any note will probably be fully extolled, and in a manner more satisfactory to the owner than the author is capable of doing.

CARE OF THE RIFLE.

Most men need no caution about taking care of the rifle. Its cost, beauty, and its response to calls to duty, all enhance the affection with which a gentleman regards his rifle. A man who will put his rifle away dirty, or defer its cleaning to a more convenient time will never shoot well. One experiment will prove the author's idea and cost the price of a new rifle. Ten minutes will prove sufficient time to enable the rifleman to clean and oil the barrel, action and lock thoroughly. Two or three *fooling shots* less, after the close of a string, will give ample time to clean up before you have to run for the train.

SIGHTS.

Open or military sights, as at present made, lack even the appearance of genius that a savage might be expected to employ in their manufacture. There is no evidence, certainly in the sights, that a civilized individual ever gave their improvement a thought. The fact that many off-hand shots have been successful with them, reflects no credit upon the maker of the sights, but rather challenges the admiration of the world for their skill.

The same intelligence that a private soldier is required to employ in moving the slide of the rear sight to the required elevation could be applied in moving the rear sight right or left as a wind guage—especially, if (contrary to the sighting of all military rifles now) when moved up or down, right or left, the sights would cause the rifle to send a bullet on its proper course. The sight is too far from the eye and too cumbersome. Henry Ward Beecher once said, "Place a privilege in a man's hands and he will learn to enjoy it;" so the author says, place decent sights in a private soldier's hands and he will soon learn their use. How to use what we have is the subject for our consideration. For off-hand shooting, the lowest part of the middle of the back notch, the top part of the front sight and the white just under the bull's-eye, form a proper line of sight for a clear, still day.

For mid-range shooting the prone position is exacted with a military rifle. Invert the sliding bar of the rear sight, which then presents a flat surface; determine what *point* of the flat surface, always toward the wind, will be desirable to properly align the front sight and the white just under the bull's-eye with *it*, thus making allowance for wind; the sight having been previously blackened with the smoke of burning rubber; draw the file of your knife blade over that point just the least bit; a small bright spark will show which enables the eye to take the finest sight. A Vernier scale for guaging elevations with the sliding bar should be used. *Be careful to hold the rifle plumb.*

Sporting, *i. e.*, hunting guns are ornamented (?) with all kinds of hybrid sights, each one of the many requiring especial study as to how it can best be used.

Fine rifles, only, seem to have had proper attention in regard to sights.

Fine Vernier sights are *the* thing. Much improvement has been made in them in the last year. The Robbins-Madison Vernier and wind-guage combined, and Sharp's new Vernier are excellent.

The fine foreign Vernier sights are so divided that they can be used on the handle or butt of the stock with the same elevations; the divisions for the butt being proportionately larger, or assimilated divisions. Wind guages are necessary and should be made in hundredths of inches. Always screw the *barrel towards* the wind.

Spirit levels are as necessary as the sights, for if the rifle is not plumb the trajectory describes a side instead of its top curve and the bullet falls right or left low.

Above all, see to it that your wind guage block is centered properly, that is, so that if there is no wind, the wind guage stands at zero; that *it* is

16   MODERN OBSERVATIONS ON RIFLE SHOOTING.

plumb; that the Vernier is plumb; and that when they are plumb with *each other* and *the rifle*; that the *spirit level* is plumb with *all*. Front sight discs are made in great variety of patterns. Open bead supported by one, two, three, and four prongs; open bead and bar; split bar or Goodwin bar; callaper, fine, medium, and coarse; pin-head; and many others varying with the imagination and fancy of man. The open bead is more generally used by the Americans than any other. The bar-bead and callaper are used to advantage by some of our best riflemen.

The Australians use the pin-head, triple callaper and bar-bead. The Scotchmen use the Goodwin bar and pin-head, and the Irishmen mostly the Goodwin bar. The author recommends the pin-head for off-hand work and the open-head for fine work; the latter sight can be varied in size of aperture and thickness of metal surrounding the aperture. The bar-bead covers the lower portion of the target. That sight which gives the eye an opportuity to see the bulls-eye plainly in position, and at the same time to casually observe the balance of the target, is in the author's opinion the best. Do not use a sight that compels the eye to be a judge of quantity of white allowed above, below or on either side of the bull's-eye, as you will be interfering with the uses for which the Vernier and wind-guage are especially employed.

SHADES ON THE SIGHTS.

It is allowable and fair to have shades over your sights on fine rifles. By all means procure them and have them nice. The spirit-level above all should be shaded, as the eye can then see it to much better advantage. Shades are not necessary when the sky is, and is likely to remain, overcast.

SHELLS.

Brass shells are the best under all circumstances. Steel shells have been tried fairly and condemned on account of cost, liability to split if they do not fit the chamber accurately, etc. Short shells, holding the powder, with one-eight of an inch to spare for seating the ball, are the best.

Not enough care is bestowed on cleaning shells. A residuum sweats the shell and dampens the new charge. Verdigris, in any portion of the shell, kills the gas of the burning powder and causes the bullet to drop low. Especially is verdigris in the cap holes fatal to good shooting. Warm water, a good brush and manual labor, backed up with plenty of ambition, will clean shells; then dry thoroughly in an oven, and finally wipe them well inside and out with a dry cloth.

See that the cap holes are free, that the anvil (if so objectionable a thing is used) is in its place, and then seat the cap home below the level of the shell-head. All acids should be avoided.

POWDER.

Muzzle-loaders, with no breech action to be strained, needing clean powder, using hard bullets, burn lightning powder to advantage.

Breech-loaders, that can be cleaned after each shot, burn slow powder to the best advantage; the powder, acting with gradual accelerating force, does not strain the action.

In last year's edition the author endeavored to give relative elevations for the powder then generally used. Experiments which have been made within the year attest the earnest endeavor of the powder manufacturers to grow apace with all other improvements calculated to produce perfect results. Of course the great variation in the different lots of powder made upset to-day rules made yesterday; especially when comparing one company's powder with another. There is a greater variation among shooters as to what suits their special desires, consequently a greater number of makers and brands swell the number of comparative elevations to such proportions as to fairly put it out of the author's power to do the subject justice. Perhaps no one man has made or can make all the experiments necessary to exhaust the list. The writer will always gladly give any information asked for, gleaning it from the best sources, if it is not already in his possession.

Keep your powder dry, *always*, the moment it gets damp it loses strength and evenness of quality, no matter how dry it may become subsequently. The thousand and one ways in which powder will gather moisture need not become a matter of experiment—simply and absolutely dry it must be kept.

The capacity of rifles to burn powder is widely different, some rifles reducing elevations until 110 grains have been used, while others do not change elevations for any amount over 95 grains. Find the capacity of the rifle and then use two or three grains more. In putting the powder in the shell, a tube from six to thirty inches long should be used through which to pour the powder; falling this distance it packs in the shell evenly; 105 grains can be put into a medium shell easily. A short shell with 100 grains are recommended for general use.

As long as the rifle will burn the powder 1 point for 1 grain should be allowed in elevation at 800, 900, and 1,000 yards.

BULLETS.

There is no doubt that every rifleman desires some improvement in bullets for breech loaders. With slow powder, hard bullets do not always upset; *i. e.* take the grooves evenly. Soft bullets lead (led) more freely than hard ones; and, while all of them may go on the target, they do not average as close in to the center as hard ones. Hard bullets, while measuring better on the target, are liable at times to miss entirely. Nearly every make of rifle has its special bullet, and so to recommend any would be an unthankful task. A difference of 10 grains in the weight of bullets calls for 1 point more or less elevation; this fact is a sufficient suggestion as to the importance of weighing bullets as well as powder.

There seems to be a constant desire existing, on the part of riflemen, to patch bullets better than they are patched at the factory. While there may be some little carelessness in properly performing this work, consequent on the ever absent sympathy between workman, or rather workwoman, and rifleman; and heightened by conversation, lunch-hour, late evening parties, etc, there is present, a *habit* of doing this special work, that is to greater advantage than the rifleman's personal interest and close attention. To supplant the paper used is another opportunity for experiment. It is not the author's desire to curtail such innocent amusement, but every rifle-maker in the country is doing his best to better the present patching and far more scientifically than shooters can do it.

In loading shells, care should be taken that the bullet fits the mouth of the shell, not too tight not too loose, that the bullet is seated just so far as another bullet, no farther. It is *not* strictly necessary that the bullet touch the powder—still too great a vacuum should be avoided.

One-eighth of an inch is recommended as far enough to seat the ball. Use the ball-seater only to straighten the bullet in the shell.

WADS.

For muzzle-loaders the Rigby and Metford wads are the best and only thing that should be used.

For breech-loaders NO WADS whatever should be used. The bullet should be seated directly on the powder.

LOADING IMPLEMENTS.

The loading implements, mentioned in OUTFIT FOR LONG-RANGE, need but little attention here. Invention, common to our country, has given us the best. The instrument for extracting the cap and replacing it with a new one is perfect.

A shell crimper can be made by any machinist. A piece of steel one inch thick with a round hole of less calibre at one end than at the other is good enough; the difference in calibre should not be too great.

A ball starter should be a piece of steel capable of just fitting in the hole of the shell crimper, for spreading open the mouth of the shell, with a convenient handle.

A ball seater is a piece of steel containing an exact duplicate of the chamber of the rifle and a portion of the barrel, with a plug sufficiently distant from the chamber, so that when the cartridge is made it can be inserted in this false rifle, seating the ball in the shell and straightening it. It is claimed that ball seaters are now made to perfection.

The funnel with tube can be improvised out of a tin whistle if necessary, care being taken to have the end of the tube crimped in or out, so that it will fit the mouth of the shell perfectly without entering it. The tube may be six or thirty inches long to suit requirements; the longer the tube the closer the powder will pack.

Scales and weights can be bought anywhere, but the author recommends the use of a fine article.

Mr. J. P. Waters, Assayer, No. 12 John St., N. Y. City, who is deeply interested in the art of rifle-shooting, and who is extremely courteous, has given the author permission to refer riflemen desiring something nice in this line to him; he will have scales and weights made to order for you and without charge for his services.

TABLES FOR WEIGHTS AND MEASURES.

AVOIRDUPOIS WEIGHT.

Drachms.
16 = 1 oz.
256 = 16 = 1 lb.
7168 = 448 = 28 = 1 quarter.
28672 = 1792 = 112 = 4   "   = 1 cwt.
573440 = 35840 = 2240 = 80   "   = 20 "   = 1 ton.
144 lbs. Avoirdupois = 175 lbs. Troy.
1 drachm   "   = 27$\frac{1}{8}$ grs. " or Apothecaries weight.

TROY WEIGHT.

24 = 1 dwt.
480 = 20   "   = 1 oz.
5760 = 240   "   = 12 "   1 lb.
Grains.

APOTHECARIES WEIGHT.

Grains.
20 = 1 scruple.
60 = 3   "   = 1 drachm.
480 = 24   "   = 8   "   = 1 oz.
5760 = 288   "   = 96   "   = 12 "   1 lb.

The pound, ounce and grain are the same in Apothecaries and Troy Weight. In the former, the ounce is divided into 8 drachms, the drachm into 3 scruples, and the scruple in 20 grains.

7,000 grains, Troy, = 1 lb. Avoirdupois.
437$\frac{1}{2}$ "   "   = 1 oz.   "

The above table will be found very useful in weighing out powder and bullets to load and reload cartridges.

1 lb. of Powder will fill 100 50 calibre, 70 grain Cartridges.
1 "   "   "   90 44   "   77   "   "
1 "   "   "   77 44   "   90   "   "
1 "   "   "   73 44   "   95   "   "
1 "   "   "   70 44   "   100   "   "
1 "   "   "   66 44   "   105   "   "

Bullets for 50-70 cartridges, weigh 17$\frac{1}{2}$ to the pound.
"   " 44-77   "   "   16$\frac{1}{2}$ "   "
"   " 44-90   "   "   12 8-11 "   "

LOADING AMMUNITION.

Fixed ammunition should have as much care in its preparation as any other detail necessary to good shooting.

Shells should be used but twice in the majority of breech-loaders; there are rifles, however, that will admit of the use of shells many times.

The shells must be absolutely clean.

The shells should be crimped or expanded at the mouth so that the bullets will fit uniformly.

The mouth of the shell should be smooth, so as not to cut the paper on the bullet.

Where the head of the shell swells or springs when fired for the first time, before recapping, put it in the ball-seater and, placing a piece of wood over it, to guide and receive the blow, strike it until the head of the shell is sufficiently flattened.

The cap should be seated deep; first, to make sure that it will explode; second, to have it below the head of the shell to avoid accident.

A scratch mark should be made on the shell to enable the shooter to insert it in the rifle the same every time, the scratch mark being on top. The shell will the better fit the chamber when subsequently used.

The powder should be weighed accurately, one charge right after the other, and carefully poured into the shell through a tube, with nothing to employ the mind until all the charges are weighed.

Weigh the bullets carefully, assorting them so that enough will be found of one weight for a day's work or at least for one range. With a lead pencil mark how far they are to be inserted in the shell. Insert them carefully with the fingers, the better to be assured that the paper is not torn or ruffled up; then, with the ball-seater, straighten them.

Carefully pack them in little boxes, that will contain 5 or 6 each, with paper or cloth to avoid shaking in transportation.

Never have two or more kinds of ammunition in your box so that you can possibly mistake one for the other during a score.

LOADING THE RIFLE.

The rules of all well-regulated ranges are explicit in their injunctions as to putting the cartridge in the rifle. NEVER load a breech-loader except at the firing point, and then keep the muzzle towards the target. No possible amount of regret could ever repair the damage if by chance your rifle should ever once cause an accident. Many riflemen, on finding a cartridge fit tightly, seek a stump, and, grasping the hammer with their fingers, strike the breech block on the stump driving the cartridge into the chamber. The firing pin is in the center of the breech block; should it get caught and hit the cap, or should the cap be flush with the head of the shell and the breech block set it off, disaster must ensue, for there is no support for the breech block, which cannot be locked till it is closed. This is true of more than one kind of rifle.

The muzzle-loader requires to have the powder weighed or measured carefully; the best method is probably to weigh the charges and put them in little glass phials—the bullets are specially prepared and do not vary much in weight. Oiled wads, which are intended to clean and lubricate the barrel, are manufactured expressly for muzzle-loaders. Press the bullet home carefully and, if conscious that the paper is disturbed in pressing it down, discharge the piece in the dirt and reload. A mark on the rod will indicate when the ball is home.

CLEANING.

To describe the diversity of methods used in cleaning would be a task without equitable results.

First—Water should be used freely on a brush to rinse out the residuum of the powder. The brush should have a wooden rod to be used for nothing else.

Second—Dry flannel or Canton flannel rags should then be used with a slit rod so that the rags pass through and out and return, thus wiping the muzzle and avoiding the return of a bare rod, as in the case of a rod with a button. Continue wiping till the barrel is clean.

Third—A flannel rag saturated with oil should be used in another slit rod, same as dry rag, until the barrel is well oiled.

Fourth—A fresh, clean rag in another slit rod should be used to wipe out the oil. Habit will soon control this last wiping so that the barrel will be left uniformly clean.

A rifle will not lead (led) when cleaned as above.

A rifle will lead at times when not cleaned as above.

Four rods are necessary, and no more cumbersome than one.

Be careful that there is no metal on any rod in such a position as to scratch the barrel.

Lance wood rods, while more costly at first, last longer, have greater strength for less thickness and are nicer in every way than any other.

Don't let any one inveigle you into the lazy habit of "a rub and a go." You might just as well shoot out of a muzzle-loader and thereby save much more trouble. Men who are too lazy to clean out their rifles, thoroughly, will draw a picture of their laziness on the target, if perchance the bullets all get there. Too much oil or water in the barrel is only a different kind of dirt.

OIL.

Never use sweet or olive oil. Never use kerosene oil. Sperm oil and sewing-machine oil are the best. The latter can easily be procured at any sporting emporium.

Rigby and Metford wads used in loading are also full of oil for lubricating these famous muzzle-loaders. Some riflemen use them to lubricate breech-loaders. They are not intended for, and do not subserve the purpose as well as oiled rags.

POSITION.

In endeavoring to favor certain positions the writer is not unaware of the difference in the formation of men. What will suit one cannot suit another. The author is free, however, to state what positions should be avoided. Do *not* put the butt in the *left arm pit*, the shock will affect the *heart*. Do not recline the head on the stock in such a way that the recoil or bound will jar the head—injury to the head and poor shooting at the last range will be certain. Do not hold the butt plate in the hand on the side from which the shot is fired, the arm being twisted in an unnatural shape will soon tire out and cause unsteadiness, and the recoil often times gets the better of the hand, causing the sights to strike the eye. Lastly, do not waste any time experimenting with a fine rifle in the prone or front position. It is safe to aver that the next International match will find all of America's opponents on their backs. The "Farquharson" position, commonly known as Fulton's position, is made up by bending the right knee about the left ankle, thus forming a crotch to support the barrel, the stock, passing by the head over the right shoulder, is seized at the butt plate by the left hand, the head resting on the left fore arm, the right hand at the trigger. This position is varied by grasping the thick of the barrel with the left hand and resting the head on the stock, the recoil or rather bound is too severe for the head, and the hand does not always hold the recoil with the same degree of firmness. This latter position is still further varied by turning the body well over on the right side, the barrel resting on the left thigh. The objections remain the same. The position adopted by the Australian Team, said to have been first used by Fraser of the Scottish Team, is somewhat varied by different marksmen, and is the strongest position. The legs disposed as in the Fulton position, the butt of the piece resting in the right arm pit, the left hand supporting the head, right hand at the trigger. General Dakin varies this by putting the left hand behind the butt plate in the arm pit, the hand serving as a cushion to check the recoil. Allen uses the left hand at the swell of the barrel, pulling the butt into the right arm pit to reduce the chance for recoil. With these latter positions, the Vernier sight can be placed on the heel of the butt lengthening the leverage of sight. The Milner position is strong, with the exception that it is a very low one, the toe of the butt must almost touch the ground (see Mirage). The knees bent to the left allow the

MODERN OBSERVATIONS ON RIFLE SHOOTING. 23

barrel to rest on the toes of both feet, the butt well in the arm pit, the left hand on the stock to plumb the piece, the right hand at the trigger.

Do not change locality at which you lie down during a score; ten feet nearer to or further from the target will change elevation one half point or more.

OFF-HAND AND MID-RANGE WITH OPEN SIGHTS.

The following rules, written some time since by the author, and styled A, B, C's, are simple, terse and seem to cover the ground thoroughly :

RULES.

Stand erect on both hips, feet at right angles conveniently apart and firmly planted.

Press the butt against the shoulder with both hands, the left hand grasping the piece firmly at or in front of the lower band. The left elbow under the piece, the right at the hight of the shoulder.

In issuing the first edition the author asked for criticism. The offhand position is the only portion of the text objected to. The author admits that some fair shooting has been done with the elbow against the body but claims his position best, not only on its merits but, by every authority extant. With some the arm extended works still better.

The lower part of the middle of the back notch, the top part of the front sight and the white just under the bull's-eye, forms a proper line of sight for a clear, still day.

If the wind blows across the range aim a little toward the direction the wind comes from.

Stop breathing when about to fire.

Pull off with the second joint of the second finger, pull slowly till the piece fires; a jerk will spoil the shot and oftentimes pull clear off the target. If the shot goes off the target to the right aim to the left of the bull's-eye to counteract the error. It would be better to amend the error of pulling off which alone causes the difficulty. Keep the eye open and observe the aim until after the shot is fired, a flinch or fear of the explosion will enhance the kick of the piece and demoralize the nerves. Practice in aiming and pulling off without cartridges should always be had at the firing point before firing. The sights should be so arranged, temporarily for this practice, that after pulling off, the aim can still be maintained ; any deviation on account of firing can thus be noticed.

The author has no kind words for the kneeling position. With breechloaders, troops should be allowed to lie down, even at 200 yards. A man is better self-possessed, more sure of his aim, more safe and better under control when lying down. A man standing, with the enemy close in front is so preoccupied in loading and firing that his legs often get the better of his judgement and courage; causing him to run into unecessary danger(?)

2

The front position is demanded in military shooting. The author thinks this demand erroneous. When the enemy is retreating, a fixed rest and certain aim, even at the cost of an instant of time, is better than supporting the body as well as the rifle on the arms. When it comes time for retreat the rifleman can turn over from his back and run twice as quick as he can gather himself from the prone position. When he turns over from the back position, his face is in the direction whither he desires to amble. The prone position should be thoroughly studied. Short-armed men may not be able to take the position recommended by the author, but they should approach as near to it as possible.

If the target is at the north, face the north-east and lie down in that direction; strike the toes well into the ground, and settle the body down as low as possible; throw the left elbow over to the right, grasp the piece with the left hand from underneath, the fingers reaching as far around as possible; back of the hand to the right. As the muzzle of the piece is carried over to the left, to its proper alignment, it puts every muscle of the left arm on tension, and consequently there is no joint to wriggle or shake. The butt should be placed against the right shoulder, passing along and by the collar bone. The right arm is free to manipulate the piece.

To make a crotch of the two forearms, and put the piece against the collar bone, is to have the bases of that crotch on the uncertain cartilage of the elbows and the butt where it can hurt you most. In the position recommended, the left elbow is not under the piece but to the right of it. Long-armed men will grasp the piece at or near the sight rack; short-armed men near the breech.

The pull off here should be very slow and perfect. In no case should the piece be spasmodically set off, as if catching the target on the wing. Be sure to hold the piece plumb; it is easy to make a sufficient error, when not doing so, to throw the shot off of the target altogether.

SIGHTING AND WARMING SHOTS.

"Sighting shots" is a term generally employed to designate actual shots, allowed previous to the beginning of the score, for the purpose of securing elevations and windage. In long-range shooting these are being discarded so as to determine relative science in judging elements on the first shot. Never take sighting or trial shots on practice days; begin your score on your judgement and if the result is a miss, take it, and do better next time. This discipline is of incalculable value. Sighting shots, as the author would consider them, might be called snapping shots. Without a cartridge, to take position at the firing point and go through the motions of aiming and firing, determines the degree of steadiness and accustoms the eye to the sight. Many of our best shots do this, without ever giving themselves a reason why.

Warming shots are blank or ball cartridges exploded in the gun to warm it to an even heat before beginning a score. A difference in elevation, in the first three or four shots, is found by nearly all marksmen, which is accounted for by the difference in the heat of the gun.

Snapping shots are equally as valuable as warming shots. Three blanks fired in position, aiming at the target, accustoms the eye to its work, and one ball cartridge then blown off will prepare the rifle for use. The writer holds that this precaution will obviate any change in the first shots that might not be required in the last.

Snapping shots should be taken at home. A few leisure moments spent in this way strengthens and confirms the position and vision.

AIMING.

Off-hand shooting which generally results best with open sights, often calls for the shooter to aim away from the bull's-eye. Being so near to the target, this is not so hazardous as at longer ranges where a man judges one foot, at its full measurement, on a target that is reduced in size by distance. Always have the open sights sufficiently elevated so that in aiming away from the bull's-eye it is not hidden from the view. It is always best with fine sights to make the changes on the gauges and aim dead on. If however, a rifleman insists in aiming so as to allow for any change that may take place in wind or light or shade while he is in the act of aiming, if using an open bead the bull's-eye appears in the middle and a white circle around it, covering the white on either side or top or bottom is equivalent to one point of wind or elevation. It is therefore obvious how much care should be used in holding the bull's-eye in the center of the open bead, with an equal showing of white around it.

FIRING OR PULLING THE TRIGGER.

When about to fire, inflate the lungs moderately and then hold your breath till the bullet is gone. The pressure of the finger on the trigger should be very slow and steady so that when the hammer trips the steadiness of the rifle is not disturbed.

WEATHER.

All other things being equal, a cloudy, moist, warm day gives lowest elevation; and a hot, bright day, or a very cold, bright day, highest elevation. In the first instance there is no mirage, the eye is comfortable and lubrication is freer, *i.e.*, the residuum of powder in the barrel is soft; on the hot day the eye is strained, mirage constant, and the powder cakes in the barrel causing friction and often causing the barrel to lead (led) from the bullet. These general rules are more or less modified by wind direction, season of the year and condition of the ground, if wet or dry. At times fog settles like a wet blanket, often totally obscuring the target. Plenty of time in sighting will give less variable results than raising or lowering elevations, as the fog is more or less dense.

MIRAGE.

Careless observers, even, have noticed that heat rising from a stove causes the atmosphere to dance, and distorts images behind it; so casual observers notice on a sunny day that between them and the targets there is a dancing of the atmosphere. A powerful telescope becomes almost worthless from the fact that this dancing appears to assume the consistency of a river running by. This is what some of the Irish Team of 1874 called "Gin and sugar," but is what we call mirage. To penetrate this consistency of the atmosphere, according to science, with set rules, has not as yet been attempted, although no one will be found unwilling to acknowledge its importance. A cock of hay in front of the bull's-eye will send up enough mirage to join it to the bull's-eye, making it impossible to take sight. A cloud covering the range will entirely disperse the mirage, so we must admit that the sun's rays are necessary to produce mirage; as the heat rising from a cock of hay does not stop rising on account of a cloud, but because there are no sun's rays to refract, we are unable to see the heat and it no longer serves as an obstacle. After securing elevation, mirage indicates its intensity or diminution best through a fine telescope. Set the glass on four legs, put together on the principle of a saw horse. Set the cross hairs so as to cut the exact center of the bull's-eye. The bull's-eye will appear to lower as the mirage increases, and rise as it diminishes. If the bull's-eye lowers so that the cross hairs cut the top, four minutes more elevation are required; that is to say, each 4½ inches (actual) of the bull's-eye *above* or *below* the *cross hairs*, indicates one minute less or more of elevation. In other words, each ¼ of the bull's eye, as cut by the cross hairs, equals one point of elevation. Mirage disappears when a cloud covers the firing point and 300 yards toward the target. Should the sun shine on this portion and shade cover the entire balance of the range, including the target, the mirage is not interfered with. Should the first instance occur, with bright target, less elevation is needed. Should the second instance occur more elevation is needed. Should the entire range be shaded by a dark cloud the absence of mirage equalizes the darkness as to elevation; plenty of time being taken in sighting. Bright sunlight succeeding reauires much less elevation, for the time, mirage coming on again requires a slight creeping up in elevation. The lower the line of sight the more dense the mirage. The rifle can be sighted much better at the height of the shoulder than on the ground. The writer holds that all low positions fail perceptibly on days when the mirage is dense enough to be an obstacle at all.

EYE.

In no treatise on rifle practice, as yet known, has the eye received the least consideration. In making so extended a paragraph the author desires to develop criticism and thereby develop experiment on this very essential feature. It is a fact, that in warm weather, grey and blue eyes make better shooting than dark eyes. In pronounced cold weather the difference is not as marked, still very few dark eyed men have achieved success as marksmen. All of the members of the American teams have been light-eyed men.

Shooting from the same position a dark hazel eye requires $1\frac{1}{2}$ minutes less elevation at 1,000, yards than a blue or grey eye. It it safe to assert that no marksman has yet been known with a black eye—(unless we except a few temporary ones belonging to riflemen whose peculiar positions have caused them—of one of these positions, one of the Scottish team remarked, that "he looks like a crab on a skewer.") There must be a reason for all this, and it is a natural as well as a philosophical conclusion that the less dense the iris the less the variation of the pupil. On this principle, also, are we to to account for variation in elevation consequent on light and shade. We have only to recall the fact that the pupil of the eye, opens and closes to a greater or less extent to accustom itself to each new object to give force to the idea that each shot should have a uniform time given to its sighting; and that the eye should traverse the same objects, as nearly as possible, between shots, to retain for it an equal power of vision. An exaggerated example may draw attention to this topic more forcibly, viz.: no one can look at grass for some time and then suddenly look at the sun and endure the light any more than he can, after becoming accustomed to the intense sunlight, turn to mundane objects and see them clearly at once. On a very bright day it is not unnatural for a marksman when awaiting his turn, to look at the very bright target, while before the very next shot he might find himself looking at the ground, or at his score book, or at a brother marksman. Such opposites must be avoided. The author claims as part proof of the above that elevations are not as bothersome on cloudy days as on bright days. Perhaps the best way to control the whole matter is for the rifleman to observe a certain interval, after he has properly obtained sight and before he pulls the trigger, to allow the eye to become fully assured of its observation. In this way, better than any other, can the marksman lessen the influence of fleeting clouds. It is a fact, though disputed by some, that, on a bright warm day, a heavy cloud covering the range calls for more elevation, unless the eye is given ample time to penetrate the darker atmosphere; and the change is more marked, when the cloud, after obscuring the range for a few minutes, passes away and renews the bright light. The writer holds that *then* every rifleman must lower elevation.

It often occurs, on days when fleeting clouds are the rule, that as the marksman has found his aim and is about to pull off, the bull's-eye leaves the sight, notwithstanding the fact that he is, and that he knows he is, holding perfect. Beware of following this *Ignus Fatui* too quickly; for, while the eyes see differently, the target has not moved. Shutting one eye is getting out of date as it develops one eye to the exclusion of the other, and causes nervous twitching, especially in hot weather. A leather screen or other contrivance will shut off its vision, so the eye not in use can remain open.

The use of eye glasses should be avoided. Spectacles are but little better; while the snobbish single eye glass is not only in very bad taste but fatal to decent shooting. Colored glasses, that simply shield the eye from bright light, counteract their usefulness by a percentage of loss equal to if not greater than the gain.

There is probably no influence of greater benefit to short sightedness than long-range shooting.

LIGHT.

In order to a proper understanding of the influence of light on rifle shooting, the reader will have to give close attention to the articles on EYE and MIRAGE. Some hints are necessary on the general topic. Could a rifleman select the peculiar light best adapted to his success and comfort he would choose a dull gray light natural to a completely clouded, but not threatening sky. A very bright light tires the eye and produces mirage. That light which permits the full power of a fine telescope is the best and most regular. Rain-light is preferable to sunlight. Sunlight calls for almost constant and sometimes radical changes in elevation. An entire score may be fired without changing elevation in the absence of sunlight.

In figuring up the elevation at which to begin a score light should be given a prominent consideration.

WIND.

All publications extant make an enormous bug-bear of wind, and the young rifleman has thus far felt that, if he did not screw his wind gauge out of all correspondence with his previous shot, he would certainly miss the target, and make himself a target for the jests of his companions. The distance covered by the ball makes the opportunity for wind currents to equalize their force. What may appear to be stronger at 200 yards distance, is balanced by less force at 500 yards; so, before learning

MODERN OBSERVATIONS ON RIFLE SHOOTING. 29

any other rule, learn this: BE SLOW TO ALTER YOUR WIND GAUGE.

Wind—Direction is marked by the clock dial, the shooter standing at 6 o'clock, the target at 12 o'clock. A 3 o'clock wind is blowing from the right, a 7:30 o'clock wind from the left rear, and so on.

Wind—Force is kept by the letters A, B, C, D, E, F, marking a gentle, moderate, fresh, strong breeze, a half gale, and gale. The wind gauge is kept 5 L or 5 R as the *barrel* is moved *toward* the *left* or *right*. The number of points of wind desirable can only be estimated after finding the direction and force; for, if the wind be blowing a gale from 12 or 6 o'clock, no windage is needed (except to cover the drift, which is enhanced by a rear wind); while a 3 o'clock gale might require 15 points of windage. A wind that holds from 8 to 10 o'clock; or 2 to 4 o'clock, offers less opportunity for skill than one from 10 to 2 or 4 to 8 o'clock. These latter are called "fish tail," and are troublesome on account of changes in elevation. A front wind, say force D, requires about 4 points more elevation than a rear wind. A strong side wind causes the ball to describe a side as well as top trajectory and needs more elevation, but not so much as to be troublesome. Five points more of side wind needs one point more of elevation.

The best way to study wind is to get a happy medium, and shoot away, pretty lively, without changing anything, making careful and honest notations of your best judgement before shooting, as to force; and after shooting, as to position of hit on the target. Errors can thus be accurately corrected. Above all, when aiming, be careful not to let the wind *blow up* without noticing it, and, the first thing after shooting observe the wind—*the wind in which* YOU SHOT.

THERMOMETER.

This instrument is probably more valuable in indicating the condition of the metals, as influenced by heat and cold, with a view to keeping track of friction than for any other purpose. Rules that will apply in warm weather work to the contrary in cold weather. In Summer, with the heat at say 90°, the ground is dry and unable to give the air its proper absorption of moisture, one 40th of its weight; the metals are more nearly assimilated and friction greater; and the metals, responding to the grateful approach of cool clouds, relax as does the human body.

A dropping of the thermometer 5° should be an indication for 1 minute less in elevation. In Winter, with a bleak cold atmosphere, the thermometer down to 40°, the atmosphere is incapable of holding more than one 140th of its weight of moisture; an increase of temperature seems to act on the metal as on the body creating a genial feeling, and, directly opposite to its effects in Summer, indicates less elevation. Do not condemn this rule on account of the contrary actions of mirage. To name dates when it would be safe to arbitrate by rule is, in our very changeable climate, hazardous. Let the rifleman be influenced by the hygrometer or his bodily comfort, diminishing elevations as the temperature changes from uncomfortable heat to cooler and from uncomfortable cold to warmer and *vice versa*. In Summer time, as evening approaches and the thermometer begins to fall and the air and moisture equalize, let elevation go down correspondingly. In the Fall and early Spring, evening comes on more rapidly and, the light growing darker and the air colder and less moist, calls for more elevation.

HYGROMETER.

The hygrometer determines the amount of moisture actually in the air. The thermometer will perform the same duty if a sufficient amount of moisture is present to be absorbed or deposited in such proportion as the heat is greater or less. Plenty of moisture in the ground is all that is necessary to secure, by known laws and a thermometer, the information given by the hygrometer. In Summer when the ground is very dry, or in Winter when a cold brisk wind is blowing, the hygrometer is necessary to adequately arrive at the amount of moisture in the air. This instrument is necessary therefore, in connection with the thermometer, in accurately determining how much allowance should be made for friction. While these rules are perfectly essential for rifles that are not cleaned, between shots, they lose much of their force; when applied to rifles that are cleaned properly, (see cleaning rifles), nearly all influence of friction being thus removed.

At 32° F. the air should contain one 160th of its own weight of moisture for every additional 27° F., the capacity of the atmosphere to contain moisture doubles.

In the revised score diagrams thermometer-dry and thermometer-wet are substituted for thermometer and hygrometer. The top line serves to indicate the thermometer proper, while the two combined serve as a hygrometer. The wet bulb always registers lower than the dry bulb. Some hygrometers are made with catgut which shortens as the air becomes moist, others are made with hair. Those made with wet and dry bulb thermometers are to the author's mind the best. Pike, Optician, is making some, specially for riflemen's use, as devised by Jackson, of the American Team.

A close remark of the weather and moisture of the ground will relieve the shooter from the necessity of having a hygrometer, especially if he uses a breech-loader and cleans it properly.

BAROMETER.

Nearly every marksman acknowledges to a fluctuation in elevations corresponding to the rise and fall of the barometer, still, few give it a prominent place in influencing their judgement. A careful study has given the writer the opinion that, whenever elevations change from unknown causes, the sequel, instead of the warning, is found in this instrument.

Nothing, but heavy clouds and bright sunlight alternated, ever produces a radical change in elevation that does not thoroughly indicate itself in the barometer; and, if a shot held steadily gains or loses slightly in elevation, instant recourse should be had to the barometer for the solution; carefully following its fluctuations the shooter need have no further trouble from that quarter.

SPOTTING THE SHOTS WITH A GLASS.

No long-range rifleman should be without a good glass. Great power is not as essential as clearness. Many small glasses are clearer and less affected by mirage than larger ones. To locate a shot by the unassisted eye and the marker's disc is too vague; a glass must be used and the exact spot hit should not only be noted, but accurately noted on the score book. Many marksmen, more egotistical than wise, favor their record by marking their shots nearer the center of the target than they actually hit. Don't ever fall into so great an error. Small wooden targets, with draughtsmen's pins numbered, are nice to have, but are no better than the target in the book.

KEEPING SCORE.

The most important of all requisites to good shooting is an *accurate* record of EVERY SHOT fired, whether fired in a score or as an experiment, or to kill time, or to shoot away bad ammunition. Months after you have forgotten such mistakes as you keep out of your book, for looks sake, you will regret it, if you cannot find the bad and the reasons, so as to avoid like disaster. Be honest *with yourself* in keeping your score book. You are not obliged to show it, if it is bad, and you will never succeed if you shoot so bad that you are ashamed to know it yourself. In keeping your elevations, if you notice that a shot is a little high or low, be slow to change unless you are sure you held the rifle perfect. *It is best to hold the rifle perfect every time;* if it takes ten minutes to get up, get rested, and try it over again. If a shot hits the bottom or top of the bull's-eye it is safe to change ½ point up or down. If a shot hits above or below the center circle, 1 point can be allowed safely, unless the error comes from light and shade, and the original conditions are restored. Be very careful of *the next shot always,* so as to make sure of the necessity of more alteration.

ALLOWANCE FOR ONE POINT IN WIND OR ELEVATION.

The table of differences, submitted below, is subject to slight changes on account of distance between the sights on the rifle, powder charge, bullet, weather, difficulty of moving the sight *exactly* one point, eye sight, etc., etc.

The difference given is for inches on the face of the target, not what it appears to be by guess work.

Grip and butt refers to where the rear sight or Vernier is located; a desired result requiring *less alteration* on the scale of a Vernier or wind gauge when the rear sight is on the handle than on the butt. Measure your divisions and allow *pro rata*, more or less, as they are greater or smaller than the divisions in the table.

TABLE OF DIFFERENCES FOR ONE POINT OF ELEVATION OR WIND.

	Divisions 1-100 of an inch, Vernier and Wind Gauge.		Divisions 1-60 of an inch, Vernier and Wind Gauge.	
Yards.	Vernier on Grip. Inches.	Vernier on Butt. Inches.	Vernier on Grip. Inches.	Vernier on Butt. Inches.
200	2	1½	3⅓	2½
300	3	2⅓	5	4
400	4	3	6⅔	5¼
500	5	4	8⅓	6½
600	6	4¾	10	7⅞
700	7	5½	11⅔	9⅛
800	8	6¼	13⅓	10½
900	9	7	15	11¾
1,000	10	8	16⅔	13
1,100	11	8¾	18⅓	14⅓

SUMMARY.

The pages inserted for keeping a summary, if properly kept, will prove invaluable. The eye, taking line after line, finds elements and conditions, noted on previous days, similiar to those that present themselves for the marksman's judgement at the commencement of a new score. To start a score by guess work, or on the advice of a brother rifleman, is unscientific and lazy, and entails incalculable disgust if perchance the guess is erroneous. Some day when you are real anxious to do well, just start a score with a "goose egg" on guess, and you will find the hinge-pins of your nervous system rather loose, to say nothing of th swearing tackle of your lower jaw—(inelegant but forcible).

DO NOT BEGIN WITH YOUR WINDAGE ON THE WRONG SIDE OR YOUR ELEVATION 5 OR 10 POINTS TOO HIGH OR LOW.

TRAJECTORY.

This is the term applied to the parabola, or line actually described by

MODERN OBSERVATIONS ON RIFLE SHOOTING. 33

the bullet consequent on the action of two or more forces, viz: the propelling force of the powder, attraction of gravitation and wind. The example used to explain the angle of hit on the target would probably be actual with 90 grains FG powder, and a 550 grain bullet at 800 yards, and is sufficiently accurate for all purposes. A bullet leaving a rifle at a velocity of (in round numbers) 1,000 feet, the first second would go 800 feet the second, and 600 feet the third, total 800 yards. At the end of the first second, the bullet would be 28 feet from the ground, 16 feet below the line of fire; at the end of the second second, it would be 32 feet from the ground, and 48 feet below the line of fire; at the end of the third second, it would be on the target, 107 feet below the line of fire. Dropping 32 feet in the last 600 feet, the angle of hit would be *one* inch fall in *twenty* inches, 3° less than horizontal.

The difference is so immaterial that it should be discarded in making allowance for faulty elevations. The slightest zephyr of wind, or difference in light, or error in holding, is more material. (For influence of wind on trajectory, see WIND.)

DIET—PERSONAL HABITS.

Little need be said on this topic; riflemen given to excesses in eating and drinking are unknown. Moderate living, very moderate drinking, including coffee, moderate tobacco, better none at all, are absolutely necessary. While it is better not to get hungry, such a condition is preferable to a full stomach. A peach, pear, or apple will quench thirst and a sandwich is all sufficient for lunch.

CLOTHING.

In warm weather bodily comfort will be a proper guide as to clothing. In cold weather an overcoat is worn until at the firing point it is discarded as too cumbersome; the result is, that the body becomes cold if not shivering. Double flannels and stockings accomplish warmth and freedom of action. Rather be too warm than chilled. Always wear heavy shoes on the range.

EXERCISE.

Plenty of moderate exercise is recommended except gymnastics.

One important thing should be fully observed—never run for a train or walk fast on the day of shooting, better turn back home and save expenses.

Never try to accomplish too much in one day, all will prove good for nothing.

EXPERIMENTING IN A MATCH.

Granting that candor rather than ill-luck has actuated riflemen in many instances within the writer's memory to ascribe their misfortunes to experiments, we can reach but one conclusion, never experiment in a match. Cartridges loaded by a friend eighty years old; bullets patched with sized paper; sights shaded one shot and minus a shade, which has dropped off the next; powder of different make, quality or quantity; powder crushed by seating the bullet too far; patches oiled, or rifled oiled in the middle of a score, and a thousand other peculiarities, all explain *bad luck* but not BAD TASTE.

CONVERSATION.

Any talking at the firing point, such as telling stories that superinduce laughter; discussions of an animated or quarrelsome character that call for serious reflection; and, especially, that excites the prejudices, will certainly interfere with good shooting.

The mind should have but one object in view, viz.: that collection of details which is necessary to make the next shot a bull's-eye. The introduction of *any* subject foreign to such details occupies the mind to the exclusion of some one of them.

Never quarrel. Never impose your excesses on others, whether resulting from good or bad luck.

PROTESTING.

Never protest against any action of a fellow rifleman. You may be misjudging his motives or his acts, and, in his mind, you may appear to be doubting his honor. He will never forget it. If anything flagrant is being done, that is interfering with YOUR success, quietly call the attention of the official in charge and allow HIM to take the responsibility of rectifying the matter.

Never yield a shot, if honestly in doubt, where *it* can affect *your score* so as to secure a *prize* or *requisite standing*. You are entitled to contest a shot not scored by the marker, and no honorable rifleman will find fault if you seek what *you believe to be right*. Be slow to contest shots while you are yet young in rifle practice. Beginners are always complaining of bad markers.

ALWAYS TRY TO PUT YOUR BULLET WHERE THE MARKER CANNOT FAIL TO FIND IT.

DELAYING A TARGET.

A large majority of all contested shots end in "goose eggs." Few instances occur wherein contested shots if allowed would alter results. Remember that while you are in dispute you are delaying the target; you are losing track of elevations, wind, &c.; your gun is getting cooled off; and you are disturbing your equilibrium of mind, and making your comrades on that target equally miserable.

SHOOTING ON THE WRONG TARGET.

The worst delay that you can be guilty of is putting your bullet on another target. A bullet so put almost invariably hits the bull's-eye, making your loss five points, giving the adversary then firing on that target a choice of, say, his outer and your bull's-eye, and may result in blinding the marker, and keeping that target idle, with the danger flag in front for over half an hour.

COACHING.

Politeness demands that you do not bother other marksmen with questions, which, if properly answered, would assist you to defeat them.

Generosity demands that when you are interrogated you answer to the best of your ability.

Cautiousness demands that you should couch your answer so as to relieve you of any suspicion if the information should fail to bring success.

If you are keeping a comrade's score for him offer no suggestions until they are called for.

If a comrade is keeping your score, be free to tell him, beforehand, what suggestions, if any, you desire him to make from time to time.

If you are being "coached" submit entirely to the judgment of the "coach;" improving the opportunity to correct your ideas with his success, or to note the reasons for his errors.

BORROWING.

It is unpleasant just as you are going to the firing point to have a comrade "sing out" for a screw driver, oil can, ball seater, or to ask what o'clock it is, or how the barometer or thermometer stands, &c. Every-shooter should have his own kit.

REASONS FOR ALL FAILURES.

To undertake so grave a task, as is indicated by this caption, is not self imposed. Challenged and requested, the author remembers that he started to write with a free hand; so, like a line of battle, with only a knowledge that the enemy is somewhere in front, we will commence firing, let the shots fall where they may, always hoping that some will take effect.

RIFLES.—Too deep rifling, worn out rifling, badly chambered, effect escape of burning gas, *un*uniform rotary motion of the ball, and uneven upsetting of the bullet.

SIGHTS.—Jumping of the sights during the recoil of the previous shot, the screw not being tight enough, sights not properly plumbed, causing wind-gauge or Vernier to act laterally, screwing the wind-gauge to the wrong side.

SPIRIT LEVEL.—Not properly sighted.

CAP.—Uneven action on account of verdigris, &c.

SHELL.—Improperly cleaned.

POWDER.—From moisture, verdigris or foul shell.

BULLET.—Badly seated in the shell, paper ruffling when inserted in the shell or rifle, paper adhering to the bullet after it has left the muzzle, paper leaving the bullet before it leaves the barrel, causing the rifle to lead near the muzzle.

POSITION.—Difference in recoil consequent on positions wherein the rifle is not held firmly at the butt. A rifle recoiling without hindrance will throw a shot higher on the target than one fired from a post.

SIGHTING AND FIRING.—Of all the misses made, charge better than fifty per cent of them to this cause; thirty of the fifty per cent being attributable to pulling off, and the remainder to mistaken vision common to the best riflemen. It is often the case that, after a long effort to secure a good sighting, the shooter gets tired out, and, although not satisfied with the sight, concludes to let the shot go under an agreement with himself that he will take more pains with the next.

ANGER or excitement of any kind.

WIND, light and shade.

TIME.—Unusual lapse of time between shots.

MARKERS.—Nearly all young riflemen charge their misses to bad markers. Don't display your ignorance of the art in that way.

LASTLY.—Obey established rules and the dictation of your intelligence, and your misses will be narrowed down to a very few unaccountables, at present beyond the power of human ken.

F. WESSON'S LONG RANGE RIFLES, BREECH-LOADING.

THE BEST IN THE WORLD

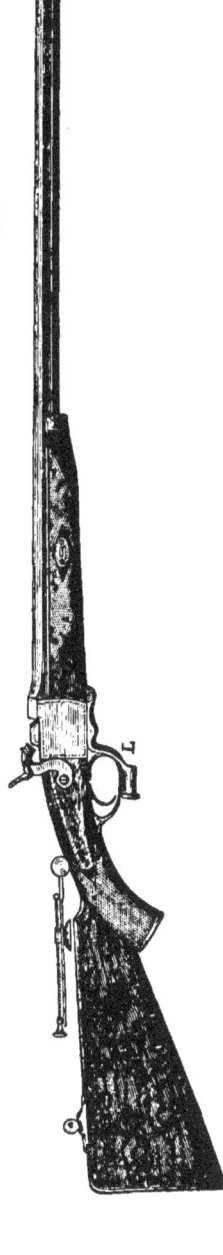

No. 1 CREEDMOOR RIFLE.

With graduated Vernier Peep Sight, interchangeable from Tang to Breech, and Wind-gauge Muzzle Sight, with Spirit Level, Stock Pistol Grip, Patent Rebounding Lock..................$125 00

ALSO

100 Central Fire Shells, Martini-Henry..........$2 50
Moulds for casting Slugs................. 5 00
Full set of Loading Tools................ 2 50
Swage for Slugs......................10 00

Mid-Range, Target and Hunting of same Action.

Also *GALLERY, SPORTING* and *HUNTING RIFLES, Old Model, of either Cal. 22, 32, 38, 44. The 38 and 44 Calibres are also made with combination Hammer to fire either Rim or Central-fire Cartridges; an important feature.*

Pocket Rifles of 22 and 32 Calibres, length of barrel, 10, 12, 15, 18 and 20 inches, the best and most perfect arm of the kind made; and at low prices. SEND FOR CIRCULAR to

F. WESSON, Worcester, Mass.

JUDGMENT OF WIND.

Some of our riflemen have a specialty of judging wind and ordinarily should be deferred to. In securing a coach, great stress should be laid on his power to cope with this wary enemy. Having one, even though not the best, his intent attention entitles him to preference in judgment.

JUDGMENT OF LIGHT.

All eyes are not affected by light equally, and it is desirable that the shooter give that individual attention, relying somewhat on the comparative difference in the effect on his eye and the shooter who precedes him. The coach only remarking on radical changes.

INSTRUMENTS.

The coach should keep a close watch on the instruments, as they affect all alike, especially where slight variations in elevation of hit are accompanied with even an indication of variation in the barometer. During very hot days the difference will increase between the wet and dry thermometer until the approach of nightfall, when it will decrease again. Not so much stress need be laid on this, as each day for weeks may serve to give an example for another, but if a shower comes on, skill with these two instruments is absolutely necessary.

ELEVATIONS.

Riflemen have heretofore paid deference to the judgment of others on right and left shooting, ignoring deviations in elevation, on the score that the previous shooter held badly. The target is twelve feet wide and only six feet tall. If a shot misses the inner right or left it may count two. If it misses up or down it counts nothing. Where the greatest percentage of loss lies, there the greatest percentage of caution should obtain.

If No. 1 goes low, in the interest of the team, he should own up if he held badly, and especially so if the next shooter is to come to grief by his error. If he claims to have held perfect, some element has changed which the coach should fathom, and allow for accordingly; failing to see any change in elements he should divide the allowance, cautioning No. 2 to hold perfect to prove the defect.

HOLDING.

In team shooting perfect holding is intensely necessary. The position should feel right or the shooter should get up and lay down again. The eye should come up to the sight comfortably, and the white surrounding the bull's-eye should be held alike through the sights each time.

PICKING A TEAM.

"Fair play is a jewel." Many interpret that sentiment in the selection of a team, as giving the idea that each man should shoot on his individual merits without coaching. If individual skill was to be the rule in the match, the ground would be correctly taken; but men who shoot on to a team in that way are liable to be contumacious throughout the shooting, for the purpose of individual record; while, if team shooting was to be indulged in in the selection, good holders and good judges of some elements, but lacking in what could readily be supplied them by a coach, would prove sufficiently tractable to submit to discipline.

To narrow down the list of competitors on the record of the first two days is an exploded idea; several days should be allowed all, and coaching should be courted, thus developing elements vastly more necessary to good team shooting than individual prowess that may never be placed to the advantage of the team.

When the number of competitors is to be reduced at all, it should be to the final number of double the number of the team, which number should stand throughout, at the same time four coaches, four spotters and four scorers should be chosen, making a sett for each target of four shooters. They should be regularly changed to different sets of fours, and each coacher's final average should determine as to coachers just as much as final average determines the team. The team should be finally chosen so as to admit of three practice days as a team entire—coach, spotter and scorer as carefully as the shooter. The captain should be chosen by the sixteen; four practice days before the final selection of the team he should immediately apply himself to finding out the different methods of loading and cleaning, submitting erroneous methods to the sixteen for consideration. The failure of any of the members to experiment properly on any improvement suggested would go far towards ostracizing him in the final selection. An Adjutant should be had to keep scores, compile them, and convey the captain's instructions. A Quartermaster should be appointed to provide transportation, meals, tents, and care for the property generally. An Instructor might act until the selection of Captain takes place.

Have Your Good Shooting Lithographed,

LIKE MADISON'S SCORE, ON PAGES 56 AND 57.

Targets can be Lithographed in Your Own Handwriting, Cheap, Quick and Handsome, by

JOHN P. SIMONDS,

53 and 55 Liberty St., N. Y.

Autograph Circulars made while you wait.

All kinds of fine Lithographing, Bank Notes, Drafts, Bill and Letter Heads, Portraits, Diplomas, Cartoons, &c.

Any competitor challenging the marking of a shot shall first deposit with the Executive Officer or his representative the sum of $1.00. If his challenge is sustained the money shall be returned. In case the challenge is not sustained the money shall be forfeited to the Association.

4. Any alteration of a scoring ticket must be witnessed by the officer in charge of the firing point, and endorsed with his initials.

VII.—RUNNING DEER.

1. Will be run only by signal from firing point. Any rifle may be used, provided the sights are without *transverse adjustment*. Position, standing; distance, 100 yards, unless otherwise prescribed. A fine of ten cents will be imposed for firing when out of bounds, not firing, or for hitting the haunch.

SCORING AND SIGNALING.

Bull's eye, white disc, counts 4.
Centre, red " " 3.
Outer, black " " 2.
Haunch, white disc, with black cross, scoring H.

VIII.—BULL'S-EYE TARGETS.

1. Bull's-eye targets will be open all the time during the Annual Meetings.

2. Tickets (entitling the holder to one shot at any Bull's-eye target) will be sold at the office of the Financial Officer, upon the Range, at 10 cents each, or twelve for $1.

3. Each competitor making a Bull's-eye will receive a Bull's-eye ticket.

4. At the close of the firing each evening, the pool receipts (less one half-half retained for expenses) will be divided *pro rata* among those making Bull's-eyes, on presentation of their tickets.

5. No person will be allowed to fire more than three shots consecutively at any Bull's-eye target, provided others are waiting to fire.

IX.—MATCHES.

1. The commencement of the Annual Meetings will be signaled by the firing of two guns, 15 minutes apart. The first will be the signal for competitors and scorekeepers to assemble at the firing points, and the second to commence firing.

2. The matches will take place, if possible, at the hour previously named. Any deviation from the programmes will be posted upon the Bulletin board, as long beforehand as practicable. *The posting upon such bulletin board will be considered sufficient notice to all competitors of everything so posted.* It should be examined by all competitors daily, both morning and afternoon, before the shooting commences.

3. In team matches, at Annual Meetings, an officer will be assigned to each of the firing points as Supervisor, and will, in connection with the Scorekeeper, keep a record of the firing; and any disagreement between such Officer and Scorekeeper will be decided by the Executive Officer, subject to appeal, as provided for in the Regulations.

4. Each team may appoint a responsible person to act as Supervisor, whose duty it shall be to see that the Rules of the N. R. A. are strictly adhered to by the team at whose target he may be assigned.

5. No practice will be allowed upon the range on any of the days of the Annual Meetings, unless specially authorized by the Executive Officer. This does not apply to days upon which special matches of the Association, or of affiliating associations or clubs, take place.

X.—ENTRIES.

A.—ANNUAL MEETINGS.

1. For all competitions open to military organizations, the teams shall (unless otherwise specified) consist of twelve from each Regiment, Battalion, Company, or Troop.

2. In all cases competitors for prizes offered to military organizations must be either officers or regularly enlisted members in good standing of the Regiment, Battalion, Company, or Troop which they represent, and shall have been such for at least three months prior to the match for which they are entered; all entries must be made for full teams.

3. Entries must be made at the office of the Association in New York City, at least *one week* preceding the commencement of the meetings, when the entry books will be closed at the office of the Association, and all subsequent entries shall be called Post Entries, and a charge of 50 per cent. additional will be imposed upon all such Post Entries.

4. Competitors who are prevented from being present at any meeting shall have the entrance fees they have paid returned after the meeting, provided that they send their tickets and give written notice to the Secretary before the day on which the prize for which they have entered has been announced for competition.

5. Competitors prevented from competing by illness will receive back their entrance fees in full, on production of a medical certificate and their entry tickets.

6. The holders of post entry tickets may be ordered to fire whenever target accommodation can be provided, but should they be precluded from competing by deficiency of target accommodation, their entrance fees will be returned to them, the Executive Officer not being able to guarantee accommodation for all such entries.

7. All entries are received upon the express condition that the competitor is to appear at the firing point at the exact time named upon his score card, and complete his score within the limitation of time prescribed, regardless of weather or any other cause.

8. The same person shall not be a member of more than one team in the same match.

9. Competitors selected to shoot in team matches, or who are detailed to shoot off a tie, at a particular hour, and who find that such engagements will interfere with their shooting in other competitions, must at once communi-

cate with the Executive Officer. These cases will be provided for *when possible,* by altering the hour; and when that cannot be done, the entry will be cancelled and the entrance fee refunded.

B.—GENERAL REGULATIONS.

1. A member of the Association entering for or shooting in a match on the range must exhibit his badge.

2. A register ticket may be transferred at any time before the firing for the match has commenced, by exchanging it at the office of the Statistical Officer for one having the name of the new holder. It is available only for the hour and target for which it was originally issued. Any erasure or alteration not initialed by the Executive Officer will render the ticket invalid.

3. No post entries shall be received for any competition after the firing in such competition has commenced, unless expressly permitted by the terms of a match.

XI.--SHOOTING.

1. Competitors must be present at the firing points punctually at the time stated upon their tickets, or forfeit their right to shoot.

2. After a competitor has joined a squad he shall not quit it until he has completed his firing, or retired.

3. No two competitors shall shoot in any match with the same rifle, nor shall a competitor change his rifle during a competition, unless expressly permitted by the terms of a match, or unless his first rifle has become unserviceable through an accident, which must be verified by the officer in charge of his firing point.

4. In all competitions confined to members of military organizations, competitors shall shoot in the authorized uniform of their corps, including waist belts.

5. In each match of the Annual Meetings, except where otherwise stated, the squad or team assigned to each target will be required to commence firing at the time named on the score card, and to continue firing at the rate of one shot per minute until the completion of the score.

6. The time for each squad to commence and close will be signaled by firing a gun every thirty minutes from 9 A. M. to 5:30 P. M., and no firing by any of its members will be permitted, except between those signals. In case a competitor, without fault on his part, has been prevented from finishing his score within that time, he may apply to the Executive Officer for further assignment, the granting of which will be in the discretion of that officer.

7. Competitors retiring from a match forfeit all claims therein.

8. *No sighting shots will be allowed in any match,* but targets will be assigned as *Bull's-eye Targets* at which competitors may practice at any time, provided such practice does not interfere with their presence at the designated time at the firing point to which they may have been assigned.

9. In all competitions restricted to military rifles the competitors shall place themselves at the firing point by twos, and shall fire alternately until they have fired all their shots.

10. In other competitions the competitors shall fire their shots alternately throughout the squad.

11. Competitors may wipe or clean their rifles during any competition, except those restricted to the use of military rifles. In competitions at more than one distance, restricted to military rifles, cleaning will be permitted between distances.

12. Whenever the danger flag is displayed, competitors about to fire will be required to open the breech block of their rifles (if breech-loaders). If they leave the firing point they must withdraw the cartridge.

13. Any competitor delaying his squad will be passed by. In no case will the firing be delayed to enable a competitor to procure a rifle.

XII.—POSITION.

1. In all matches (except those for carbines), the position up to and including 300 yards, shall be standing. The left elbow may be rested against the body, provided the little finger of the left hand is in front of the trigger guard.

2. In carbine matches the position at 200 yards, shall be standing; at 300 yards, kneeling; over that distance, in any position (as prescribed for infantry).

3. In all other matches, at distances above 300 yards, any position may be taken without artificial rests to the rifle or body.

4. One-armed competitors will be allowed to use false arms without extra support, in the standing and kneeling positions, and to assume any position in the use of military rifles, at distances above 300 yards.

5. Shots at Bull's-eye targets, at all distances beyond 300 yards, may be fired in any position, without artificial rests.

6. In all cases the rifle shall be held clear of the ground.

XIII.—TIES.

I. Ties shall be decided as follows:

A.—IN INDIVIDUAL SHOOTING.

1. When the firing takes place at more than one distance, by total score made at the longest distance; and if still a tie, and there be three distances in the competition, by the total score at the second distance.

2. By the fewest MISSES in the entire score.

3. By the fewest OUTERS in the entire score.

4. By the fewest INNERS in the entire score.

5. In handicap matches (after the preceding) by the fewest CENTRES in the entire score.

6. If still a tie, by inverse order of shots, counting singly from the last to the first.

7. By firing single shots at the longest range.

B.—IN TEAM SHOOTING.

1. By the aggregate total scores made at the different distances in inverse order.

2. By the fewest MISSES in the entire score.
3. By the fewest OUTERS in the entire score.
4. By the fewest INNERS in the entire score.
5. By the total of each round in inverse order.
6. By the competitor on each side who has made the highest score, firing five rounds at the longest distance.

II.—The names of competitors who have to shoot off ties will be posted on the Bulletin Board as soon after each match as practicable.

III.—When the ties are shot off, one sighting shot shall be allowed without charge.

IV.—Competitors not present at the firing points at the hour named for shooting off ties, lose their right to shoot.

V.—If, having forfeited their right to compete, they shall still be within the number of prize winners, they shall take any prize that may be allotted to them by the Executive Committee.

XIII.—PRIZES.

1.—Prize winners will, upon application to the Statistical Officer on the range, receive certificates, which must be given up on receiving the prizes.

2. Prizes will be delivered on the range at the close of the meeting, under the direction of the Executive Officer, unless otherwise specified.

3. All prizes not claimed within one month after the match at which they have been won, shall be forfeited to the Association.

XV.—PENALTIES.

Competitors must make themselves acquainted with the regulations, as the plea of ignorance of them will not be entertained.

DISQUALIFICATION.

Any competitor—

(a)—Who shall fire in a name other than his own, or who shall fire twice for the same prize, unless permitted by the conditions of the competition to do so, or

(b)—Who shall be guilty of any conduct, considered by the Board of Directors or the Executive Committee as discreditable; or

(d)—Who shall be guilty of falsifying his score, or being accessory thereto; or

(e)—Who shall offer a bribe of any kind to an employee—

Shall, upon the occurrence being proved to the satisfaction of the Board of Directors or the Executive Committee, forfeit all his entrance fees, be forever disqualified from competing at any time upon the Range of the Association, and shall not be entitled to have any prize won by him at the time or meeting, awarded to him.

EXCLUSION FROM FURTHER COMPETITION.

1. Any competitor who shall be detected in an evasion of the conditions prescribed for the conduct of any match, shall be ruled out of such competition.

3. Any competitor, in any meeting or match, refusing to obey instructions of the Executive Officer or his assistants, or violating any of these regulations, or being guilty of unruly or disorderly conduct, or being intoxicated, will be immediately ruled out of all further competition, during such meeting or match, and forfeit his entrance fees, and may also be reported to the Board of Directors or the Executive Committee, and be by them disqualified from use of the Range.

4. Any competitor firing when the danger flag or trap disc is shown at the target or firing point, or knowingly discharging his rifle, except at a target to which he has been assigned, or into the blowing off pits, or as may be directed by an officer, shall be debarred from all further competitions during the meeting, and shall forfeit his entrance fees. This shall not apply to a competitor accidentally firing at the wrong target when no other danger disc is up.

5. Any person discharging a rifle or snapping a cap within the enclosure, except in accordance with the regulations for shooting, may, at the discretion of the Executive Officer, be required to leave the ground.

6. Any competitor or other person found with a loaded rifle, except at the firing points and when about to shoot, shall be debarred from further competition during that meeting or competition.

7. Any person, whether a competitor or not, interfering with any of the firing squads, or annoying them in any way, will be at once expelled from the ground.

8. Any competitor discharging his rifle accidentally, either by his own want of care, or by reason of any defect in the rifle, shall be disqualified from further competition in the match.

9. Should a competitor lose his register ticket, omit to take it to the firing point, fail to attend at the prescribed hour, or give a wrong ticket, and so by his own neglect miss the opportunity given to him of competing for the prize for which his ticket was issued, his claim in regard to such competition shall be cancelled.

10. Any person firing on a wrong target will be fined $1, or be debarred from further competition; or both, in the discretion of the Executive Officer.

11.—Any competitor, being a member, who shall neglect to wear conspicuously his badge of membership in any competition, shall have his score disallowed.

12.—Any person ruled out of any meeting or competition shall forfeit all entrance fees.

XV.

1.—All regulations heretofore adopted and inconsistent herewith, are hereby repealed.

2.—These regulations shall take effect immediately.

BALLARD RIFLES.

(Cut of Long Range A 1 Rifle.)

HUNTING, SHORT, MID AND LONG-RANGE.
TARGET RIFLES.

Less Recoil than any other Rifle. Perfect Shooting Guaranteed. Target Rifles are Chambered for our new straight-shell which can be used 1,000 times.

Catalogues furnished on application.

Schoverling & Daly,

84 & 86 CHAMBERS ST., N. Y.

P. O. Box 5380.

WHITNEY BREECH-LOADING RIFLES.

CUT OF LONG RANGE RIFLE.

Military, Sporting, Short, Mid and Long-Range Target Rifles.

For Accuracy, Long Range, Light Recoil, Penetration, Simplicity of Construction, Durability, Ease of Manipulation, Materials and Workmanship they are unsurpassed.

Phœnix Breech-Loading Sporting Rifles and Single Barrel Shot Guns.

REVOLVERS OF VARIOUS SIZES.

WHITNEY ARMS CO.

NEW HAVEN, CONN.

☞ SEND FOR CIRCULAR.

The only Military and Naval Journal in the United States.

ARMY _{AND} NAVY JOURNAL.

GAZETTE OF THE REGULAR AND VOLUNTEER FORCES.

THE ARMY AND NAVY JOURNAL is recognized as the standard authority on all subjects relating to our Military Establishment—THE ARMY, NAVY, MARINE CORPS, AND THE NATIONAL GUARD.

SUBSCRIPTIONS, $6 PER ANNUM.
PRO RATA FOR SEMI-ANNUAL AND MONTHLY SUBSCRIPTIONS.

Wingate's Manual for Rifle Practice.

By Col. GEO. W. WINGATE, General Inspector of Rifle Practice, N. G. S. N. Y.

The Standard Authority on Rifle Practice, and the only Work Embodying the Results of Recent Experience.

This work, originally prepared under the authority of the National Rifle Association, has been adopted by New York, Main, Massachusetts, Rhode Island, Connecticut, and other States, and is in use in the United States Army and Navy, as a text-book on this subject.

It contains nine chapters of theoretical instruction and an appendix, in which is given the Rules of the National Rifle Association to govern Matches ; Shooting; Suggestions to Marksmen ; Positions, Standing, Kneeling, Lying ; Aiming ; Wind ; Elevations ; Light and Atmosphere ; Long Range Sights ; Rifle Associations, How to Form ; Cartridges, Selection and Management of ; Team Shooting ; Forms for Recording Practice, etc., etc.

Price, $1.50. Sent by Mail, postage prepaid, on receipt of price.

W. C. & F. P. CHURCH, PUBLISHERS,

245 Broadway, New York,

Forest and Stream

AND

Rod and Gun.

THE AMERICAN SPORTSMAN'S JOURNAL.

A WEEKLY PAPER DEVOTED TO

FIELD SPORTS, PRACTICAL NATURAL HISTORY,

Fish Culture, Protection of Game,

PRESERVATION OF FORESTS,

YACHTING AND BOATING,

RIFLE PRACTICE, AND ALL

OUT-DOOR RECREATIONS AND STUDY.

This is the only Journal in the country that fully supplies the wants and necessities of the

GENTLEMAN SPORTSMAN.

Terms, $4 a Year.   Send for a Specimen Copy

Forest and Stream Publishing Co.
111 Fulton Street, N. Y.

LOOK AT YOUR SIGHTS AGAIN, BEFORE FIRING THE FIRST SHOT.

Improvised to show how to keep the record

500 YDS   DATE *Walnut Hill Mass. June* 10th 1877
BEGINNERS SHOULD STUDY PAGES 15, 22, 23, AND 24 CAREFULLY

1,000 YDS   DATE *Creedmoor L.I. July* 18th 1877
REFER TO THE MANUAL AND IT WILL SAVE YOU TIME AND MONEY

Shot by E.H. Madison of Brooklyn

	2	3	4	5	6	7	8	9	10	11	12	13	14	15
	3	4	5	4	4	3	5	4	4					
	15	"	"	"	13	15	"	"	"					
	"	1½	2½	"	"	"	"	"	"					

∘Clock
 ear and moist
right

> Cal. SIGHT ♀ POWDER 50 gr. BULLET 300 gr.
∘Clock A.M.

	2	3	4	5	6	7	8	9	10	11	12	13	14	15
	3	4	5	5	5	5	5	5	5					
	"	"	"	"	"	-27	-26	"	"					
	3	4	5	5½	4½	5	"	"	"					

∘Clock
hvin Kling
ark

| | | | | | 77 | | | 75 | | | | | |
| | | | | | 75½ | | | 74 | | | | | |

noor SIGHT ♀ POWDER 100.GR #7 BULLET 550. 1/15

	2	3	4	5	6	7	8	9	10	11	12	13	14	15
	5	5	5	5	4	5	5	5	5	.				
½	.	"	"	"	"	"	"	"	"					
R	"	"	"	"	½	1	"	"	"					
	III	"	II	"	XII	I	"	"	"					

ear
rey
o

? 975 in.
rtini SIGHT ⊗ POWDER 100.Am.#2 BULLET 550. 1/12

THE SPIRIT OF THE TIMES

The Leading Sporting, Racing, Rifle, Hunting, Dramatic, and Musical Newspaper in the World.

28 to 32 PAGES.

Recognized Turf, Trotting, and Rifle Authority of America.

RIFLES AND MARKSMANSHIP,

By JUDGE H. A. GILDERSLEEVE.

Judge Gildersleeve is now engaged in the revision of his series of articles published in *The Spirit* last spring, and they, as well as the supplementary chapters by Cols. Bodine and Wingate, will be published in book form next month. There will be added a valuable chapter on "Trajectory and Recoil," by Sir Henry Halford, giving the results of scientific experiments on his own range. Bear in mind that Judge Gildersleeve commences with a novice, and makes him an expert in ten lessons,

Published by The Spirit of the Times. Price, Single Copy, $1.50. Clubs of Twelve or over, $1. each.

Riflemen should forward their orders at an early day.

VETERINARY DEPARTMENT

A horse doctor free to every subscriber who owns a horse or other head of stock.

Throughout the year, full accounts of Racing, Sporting, Rifle, Aquatic, Musical, Dramatic, and other events are published. During the winter months, its pages are enlivened by special communications upon topics of general interest; also, Serial Stories of great merit, and correspondence from every quarter of the globe.

Subscription Price, Five Dollars a Year.

CLUB RATES—Five Copies One Year, $21; Nine or more Copies, at the rate of $4 each, payable in advance.

GEORGE WILKES & E. A. BUCK, Proprietors.

Address, 102 Chambers Street, New York.

SPIRIT OF THE TIMES,

P. O. Box 938.

SMITH & WESSON'S REVOLVERS.

MARVELOUS IN CONSTRUCTION.   **PERFECT** IN ACTION.

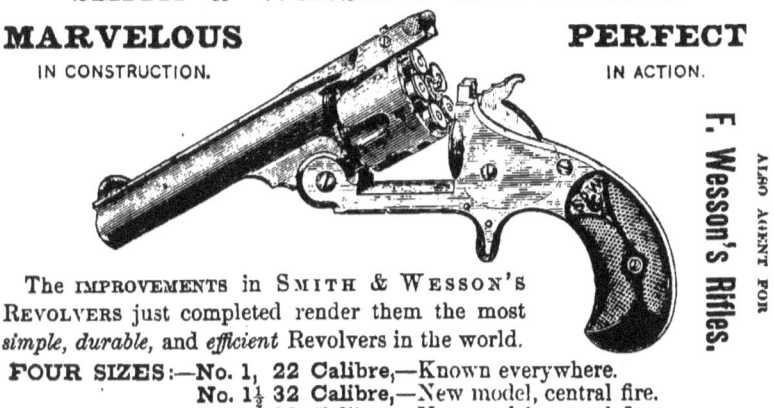

F. Wesson's Rifles.   ALSO AGENT FOR

The IMPROVEMENTS in SMITH & WESSON'S REVOLVERS just completed render them the most *simple, durable,* and *efficient* Revolvers in the world.

FOUR SIZES:—No. 1, 22 Calibre,—Known everywhere.
　　　　　　No. 1½ 32 Calibre,—New model, central fire.
　　　　　　No. 2, 38 Calibre,—New model, central fire.
　　　　　　No. 3, 44 Calibre,—Army size, Russian model.

ADDRESS, **M. W. ROBINSON, Gen. Agent, 79 Chambers St., N. Y.**

THE REMINGTON IMPROVED SPORTING AND TARGET RIFLE.

(Hepburn's Patent Action.)

E. REMINGTON & SONS,
283 Broadway, N. Y.

P. O. Box 3994.   [See Page 62.]

THE REMINGTON INPROVED RIFLE.

(Hepburn's Patent Action.)

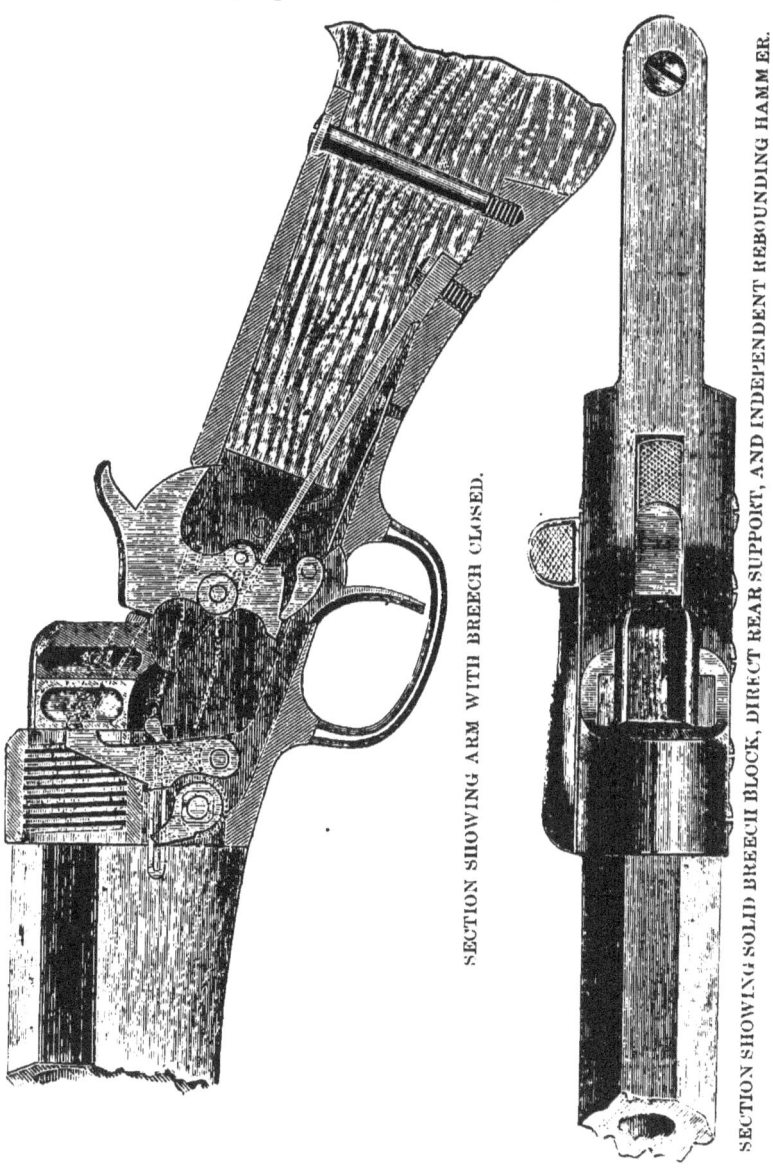

EUREKA AIR PISTOL.

Easily Loaded, Adapted for Ladies' and Parlor Use.

PRICE, including Darts, Slugs, Targets, etc.,

    Black, ... $5.00

    Nickled, ... $6.00

JOHN P. LOVELL & SONS,
Importers and Dealers in

GUNS, RIFLES, PISTOLS AND FISHING TACKLE,

Cor. CORNHILL & WASHINGTON STREETS, BOSTON.

A Splendid 7-Shot, Full Nickel Plated Revolver, only $2.50.

PEABODY-MARTINI BREECH-LOADING RIFLES.

MILITARY, TARGET AND SPORTING,

MANUFACTURED BY

THE PROVIDENCE TOOL COMPANY,

PROVIDENCE, R. I.

For symmetry of form, certainty of action, perfection of workmanship, and accuracy at the longest ranges, they are unrivalled. Our **MID-RANGE GUNS, VICTORIOUS OVER ALL COMPETITORS** at the Centennial International Short-Range Match at Creedmoor, September 12th, 1876.

But Two of our Guns used, out of One Hundred and Twenty in this Match, winning FIRST and FOURTH PRIZES.

Military Rifles of regular model, selected for accuracy, for the use of Military and G. A. R. teams always on hand.

SCHUYLER, HARTLEY & GRAHAM, Agents, 19 Maiden Lane, N. Y.

WILLIAM READ & SONS,

13 FANEUIL HALL SQUARE, BOSTON.

All our Rifles are bored expressly for accuracy, and rifled on the so-called HENRY system, which experiments in this and other countries has shown to give the most uniform results, being less liable to lead, and producing less friction than any other style of rifling in use. Send for ILLUSTRATED CATALOGUE AND PRICE LIST.

CENTENNIAL COMMISSION.—REPORT ON AWARDS.—"PEABODY-MARTINI RIFLE.

"As a Military Arm, combining strength, simplicity, high quality of workmanship, ease of manipulation, with accuracy and rapidity of fire. Using a Central Fire Metallic Cartridge, and ejecting the discharged shell unfailingly." [See next two pages.]

PEABODY-MARTINI LONG AND MID-RANGE RIFLES.

Creedmoor Pattern No. 1 Long Range Rifle

MANUFACTURED BY

Providence Tool Company,

PROVIDENCE, R. I.

Creedmoor Pattern No. 1.—Half Octagon Steel Barrel, 32 inches long; calibre 44-100; weight, just under 10 lbs.; pull of trigger 3 lbs.; stock, hand-made from extra choice black walnut, with *pistol grip*, highly polished; grip and fore end checked; sides of breech-frame handsomely engraved; peep rear sight with Vernier scale, interchangeable from *wrist* to *heel*; giving elevation for 1500 yards on wrist or 1100 yards on heel. Interchangeable globe and *open bead* front sight with wind gauge and spirit level. Price, $125.

Creedmoor Pattern No. 2—Is a duplicate of the above, except that the sides of the breech-frame are not engraved. Price, $110.

What Cheer Pattern No. 1—Is same as Creedmoor No. 2, except it has no pistol grip on stock. Price, $100.

All the above Rifles use the same cartridge, using 100 to 110 grains powder and 550 grain bullet.

For Mid-Range, and Off-Hand Shooting.—No. 1. Half Octagon Steel Barrel, 28 or 30 in. long; calibre, 40-100; weight, 9 to 9½ lbs.; pull of trigger, 3 lbs.; stock, hand-made from selected black walnut, highly polished with pistol grip; grip and fore end handsomely checked. Hollow butt plate; peep rear sight with Vernier scale; globe front sight with wind gauge and spirit level. Price, $75.

No. 2 has graduated peep rear sight; globe front sight. Price, $60. If with spirit level, $65.

The above Mid-Range Rifles are chambered for a shell using 70 grains of powder and 380 grains of lead, for practice from 500 to 800 yds., or the same shell is loaded with 55 to 60 grains of powder and 300 grains of lead, with lubricating disc in shell for hunting or practice, from 200 to 400 yards, *without cleaning.*

See page before and after this.[1]

"KILL DEER" PATTERN PEABODY-MARTINI RIFLES.

THE PROVIDENCE TOOL COMPANY,

Have just brought out a New Pattern of their celebrated Peabody Martini Rifles,

Designed to meet the wants of those who desire a rifle which shall be ACCURATE, strong, safe, not too heavy, sighted fine enough to *do good shooting up to and including* 600 *yards*, using a

Cartridge heavy enough for the Largest Game, and yet free from unpleasant recoil,

Which can be fired with great rapidity and without cleaning; well finished, easy of manipulation, and of moderate cost, and for which ammunition is readily obtained in all parts of the country. Pull of trigger, 3 lbs. Stock, hand made, Price, $40 00

Half Octagon Steel Barrel, 28 inches long. Calibre, $\frac{45}{100}$. Weight of rifle, 8 to 9 lbs. Sights, interchangeable globe and peep and open sights. from first class black walnut. Broad flat butt plate.

☞ **SIGHTS CAN BE CHANGED WHILE THE GAME IS IN VIEW.**

☞ The above rifles are chambered for the new United States Government Cartridge, straight shell, $2\frac{1}{10}$ inches long; Powder, 70 grains; Bullet, 405 grains. [See two pages previous.]

THE REMINGTON HEPBURN

LONG RANGE RIFLE.

THIS RIFLE IS DESIGNED ESPECIALLY FOR <u>LONG RANGE TARGET SHOOTING</u>, AND FOR GENERAL USE AS A SPORTSMAN'S AND HUNTER'S RIFLE.

IT HAS A <u>SOLID BREECH BLOCK WITH DIRECT REAR SUPPORT, SIDE LEVER ACTION, AND REBOUNDING HAMMER</u>, SO THAT THE ARM ALWAYS STANDS WITH THE SEAR IN THE SAFETY NOTCH, THUS RENDERING PREMATURE DISCHARGE IMPOSSIBLE, AND IS BELIEVED TO BE THE BEST IN USE FOR THE PURPOSES DESIGNATED. THEY ARE CHAMBERED FOR THE STRAIGHT 40, 44 AND 45 CALIBRE SHELLS.

E. REMINGTON & SONS,

P. O. BOX 3994.   283 BROADWAY, N. Y. CITY.

LONG RANGE TOURNAMENT.

The announcement that a match of three days' duration has been shot at long ranges, by the best riflemen in the world, is not calculated, perhaps, to startle the people of *one* continent nowadays, even though the shooting was better than any ever made, and, what is more, made on absolutely individual merit. It has been the accident of occasion that has called attention to previous matches, and we may add, properly, only by way of justice to later efforts, much more careful students and brilliant shots, that it was only the accident of occasion that caused our pioneers in long-range shooting to be so heralded for their skill, and have their names placed on the top round of the ladder of fame, thenceforth the only prophets and sages in rifle shooting. No matter what their qualifications, without claiming (in fact since then disclaiming) "even a knowledge of whether a front wind required more or less, elevation than a rear wind," only taking rifles (happily, on account of the skill of Yankee mechanism, superior to any in the world), and ammunition as furnished them, without knowing or stopping to ask how or of what they were made, they went to Creedmoor, and by luck and steady holding beat their competitors. It was all put to their credit as science. The fact was that very faulty elevations, and many unaccountable misses, developed the necessity of knowing the science of rifle shooting, and in the five or six years that have elapsed, very many of the principles underlying these errors have been established, laughed at by the mushroom sages, and the means of avoiding them finally adopted as so much gained. It is only in these few years that this subject has been brought forward as a study. Those who in 1874 stood as mountains of intelligence have since been dwarfed by the patient and careful study of many. *There is hardly a portion of* ANY *rifle then* SO PERFECT *that has not been remodeled; the ammunition is in every detail different*; changing light, heat and cold, wet and dry, barometric changes, all enter into the consideration of what shall be the elevation for the next shot. Good holding and passably judging wind currents is no longer science. Such requirements are simply necessary as adjuncts to many paramount elements of success.

Feeling the importance of collating all the information possible, and in a responsible form, thus utilizing the advancement so apparent to close observers, the Author originated the "Tournament" as the best means to accomplish the desired result. The encouragement tendered by the different rifle manufacturers and others interested in supplies, the Editors of the *Spirit of the Times, Turf, Field and Farm,* and the *Forest and Stream* and a few of the Directors of the N. R. A., who foresaw the value of the enterprise, to which, after the match began, was added the recognition of the *N. Y. Herald,* and the general approbation of all interested, have long since compensated the writer for a great amount of energy expended and opposition encountered. Every known rifle club and shooter was fully notified of the match. Answers were received from California, Nevada, Vermont, New Orleans, Mississippi, Maryland, Colorado, Canada, Wheeling, W. Va., Saratoga and all other prominent localities possessing acknowledged riflemen. Dudley Selph, Prof. Dwight, Col. Burnside, and Partello, all had a chance to contest, but were unable from some cause or other. One prominent member of a club, noted for big scores in the newspapers, did not wish to commit himself and his fellow shooters to divulging their style of loading—"something new that might not suit others, but proved successful with them." On arriving at Creedmoor, it proved that this same shooter was competing in the Wimbledon Cup Match at Creedmoor, the year previous, on the next target to the writer, and this new wrinkle was what the writer was then using, simply loading at the muzzle, using more powder than would fill the shell.

Great hopes were expressed on all hands that Partello would try to prove his prowess in this match, and he came to Creedmoor, but after two practice days left to attend his sick child. At last thirty competitors signified their intentions to enter, and the match was turned over to and adopted by the National Rifle Association.

SUPPLEMENTARY PROGRAMME
OF THE
SEVENTH ANNUAL FALL PRIZE MEETING
OF THE
National Rifle Association of America.

LONG-RANGE TOURNAMENT,
TO BE HELD UPON THE RIFLE RANGE AT CREEDMOOR, L. I.,

Monday, Tuesday and Wednesday, Sept. 22, 23 and 24, 1879

AT TEN O'CLOCK A. M., EACH DAY.

CLASS PRIZES.
CLASS I.

To the competitor making the highest aggregate score of three days, $100·

CLASS II.

To the competitor (not the winner of the next preceding prize) who, having exceeded 206 points in any match, same distances, has never exceeded 212 points in any match, same distances, making the highest aggregate score of three days, ... $100.

Prize offered by Mr. E A. BUCK, *Ed. Spirit of the Times.*

To the competitor making the second highest aggregate score, 2d Class, ... $25.

Offered by COL. E. H. SANFORD.

To the competitor making the third highest aggregate score, 2d Class, ... $15.

CLASS III.

To the competitor (not a winner of the two aggregate 1st prizes, Class I. or II.) who, having exceeded 200 points in any match, same distances, has never exceeded 206 points in any match, same distances, making the highest aggregate score of three days, ... $50.

Prize offered by JUDGE H. A. GILDERSLEEVE.

To the competitor making the second highest aggregate score, 3d Class, ... $25.

Prize offered by GEN. G. W. WINGATE.

To the competitor making the third highest aggregate score, 3d Class, ... $15.

CLASS IV.

To the competitor (not a winner of either of the three aggregate 1st prizes, Classes I., II. or III.) who has never exceeded 200 points in any match, same distances, making the highest aggregate score of three days, a Badge, Value, ... $50.

Prize offered by FOREST AND STREAM PUBLISHING CO.

To the competitor making the second highest aggregate score, 4th Class, ... $25.

To the competitor making the third highest aggregate score, 4th Class, ... $15.

OTHER PRIZES.

FIRST DAY.—To the competitor making the highest score, (45 shots), $50. Second highest do., $25. Third highest do., $15. Fourth highest, do., $10; and to each of these and the next 10 highest scores, an equal share of the entrance fees for the day, in excess of 30 entries. Total, besides entrance fees, ... $100.

SECOND AND THIRD DAYS.—Same as the first. Total, besides entrance fees, ... $200.

To the competitor making the highest aggregate score of three days, with a Remington rifle, a Remington Creedmoor Rifle. Value, . $100.

Prize offered by E. REMINGTON & SONS.

To the competitor making the highest aggregate score of three days, with a Sharp's rifle, a Sharp's Standard Long Range Rifle. Value, $100.

Prize offered by SHARP'S RIFLE CO.

To the competitor making the highest aggregate score of three days, with a Ballard rifle, a Ballard Long Range Rifle. Value, . . $100.

Prize offered by SCHOVERLING, DALY & GALES.

To the competitor making the highest aggregate score of three days, with Laflin & Rand powder, ... $50.

Prize offered by LAFLIN & RAND POWDER CO.

To the competitor making the highest aggregate score of three days, with Hazard Powder, ... $.

Prize offered by...

To the competitor making the *first completed* score in the three days, 45 shots, exceeding 219 points, ... $50.

Prize offered by (Anonymous).

If two or more scores exceeding 219 points are made in the same series of 45 shots at the three ranges, the best score to take the prize.

To the competitor making the most centers, 135 shots, one year's subscription to the *Turf, Field and Farm*, and one copy of "Perry's Green Book."

To the competitor making the most inners, 135 shots, one year's subscription to the *Forest and Stream*, and one copy of "Perry's Green Book."

To the competitor making the lowest score, 135 shots, one copy of "Perry's Green Book."

Open to all comers. 15 shots at each range. 800, 900 and 1,000 yards each day. No sighting shots. Previous practice of every description must cease at 10 o'clock. No restriction as to method of loading. *Any rifle, any position (Rules N. R. A.)* No coaching. Competitors may spot their own shots, *but no one to* CALL OUT *the location of any shot.* Scorers to be 15 ft. behind the firing points. *No one but one* competitor to be at *one* firing point at once, and *no one not a competitor in the match* to pass in front of the line of scorers on any pretext whatever. Entrance fee $5 each, each day.

Should the weather be unfavorable, the competitors present at the firing points at 9:55 o'clock *shall vote* whether to proceed or not, the majority to govern. During the shooting, if the weather shall be so unfavorable as to *prevent "aiming,"* the executive officer may suspend the shooting—not to exceed 30 minutes at any one time. Any further suspension to be subject to a majority vote of the competitors present at the time of voting. Should any portion or portions of any of the three days' scores be uncompleted on Wednesday evening, Sept. 24th, 1879, the competitors will present themselves at the firing points at 9:45 o'clock A. M. on each succeeding day, and proceed to complete said scores in such a manner as the majority of the competitors at the firing points at that time shall by vote determine, until all the scores shall have been completed or abandoned, according to the rules of the N. R. A. In starting to complete scores after Wednesday evening, Sept. 24th, 1879, one sighting shot will be allowed. Targets shall be assigned by drawing each day, and the order of shooting in each squad shall be decided by drawing at each range. Each competitor shall certify on honor, on blanks to be furnished at the firing points each day, the kind and quantity of powder to be used that day, the kind, weight and hardness of the bullets to be used that day; the kind of rifle to be used that day; if wads are to be used in loading; the kind and length of shells to be used that day; the kind of primer to be used that day; if fixed ammunition or muzzle-loading is to be used that day. Each competitor shall further certify on honor the highest score ever made by him in any match (stated prizes or subscription; association or private), in 45 shots at the three ranges. No entry will be accepted after 9:30 o'clock A. M. on any day.

	1st day.	2d day.	Total.
In 1876. The American Team, close "coaching" and shooting with all the help obtainable, made......................	1,577	1,549	3,126
In 1877. do do	1,655	1,679	3,334
In 1878. do do	1,660	*1,660	3,320

* Giving Rockwell 69 for his 1,000 yards score, and Prof. Dwight bull's-eyes to complete his score.

	1st day.	2d day.	Total.
In 1879. The Tournament, Top 8..............	1,655	1,670	†3,325

Shooting absolutely on individual merit, on different targets, no previous practice together.

† This score would have been bettered 25 points by taking best 8 each day.

While the conditions of some matches previously shot appeared to put each man on his own resources, the fact was that all the shooters were near the firing points, and that a man waiting could stand over a competitor about to deliver his shot, and give a wink, a peculiar whistle, or exclamation, which would often prove a warning. In this match the shooter was beyond all aid or hint, not even the scorer calling out a shot could be of avail as a warning. This restriction also gave the opportunity for a spectator to at once see along the line exactly who was shooting; to watch every peculiarity of the shooter at the firing point; to catch his ability to cope with the elements; and, above all, to enjoy the scene, which, instead of being huddled together and confusing, was at once graphic and entertaining.

The following letter combines so many valuable points that the author asks pardon for the digression and publishes it:

"I was feeling half sick and unfit for work when I started, but I came back feeling clear-headed and greatly improved. If business men knew the efficacy of this fascinating sport as a *means* of *recreation only* (letting scores whether good or bad take care of themselves), they would, I am sure, avail themselves of it more generally, for when used for that purpose (and not, by constant practice, to become experts) it takes no time from business which will not more than be replaced by increase of clear-headedness and *vim*. I said I went to Creedmoor for the sake of recreation; *partly*. My other reason for going was, that I heartily approved of the plan on which your 'Tournament' was organized,—that of classifying the marksmen according to their records, thereby giving inexperienced men as good a chance in their class as the more expert riflemen in theirs; and also (by extending the contest beyond one competition) that of offering prizes for single and aggregate scores, thereby affording the opportunity of redeeming the ill luck of one day by the success of the next. I hope a similar competition may be arranged for next year."

It has been the author's desire since the first publication of this book to modify any position then taken if it was proper to do so. "Retired forever" was written in the author's score book months before "Modern Observations" were prepared, on account of ill health that then had no promise of mending. In that year (1876) every shot fired by the different teams for the "Palma," both in the match and in practice, was watched by the writer.

The ammunition, style of loading, positions, sights, etc., were carefully noted, until every detail was exhausted. The writer was in constant practice (as a "coach") with others who were untiring in trying any experiments suggested. For the last two years returning health has given the author the opportunity to fill several score books, and keep pace with every improvement by personal practice. Failing to find in his own experiments, or the experience of others, any good reason for changing rules already laid down, the "Long Range Tournament" was projected as a sure way to modify or confirm "Modern Observations." The following tables show the result, and when compared with the targets selected on account of elevations, offer opportunity for scientific deduction as to the methods most liable to produce the best elevations.

Tabular Statement of conditions, scores and prize resultant from the

Place of mer't	Name	Best score ever made	Class	Scores 1st Day 800 900 1000 Tot'l Prize	Scores 2nd Day 800 900 1000 Tot'l Prize	Scores 3rd Day 800 900 1000 Tot'l Prize	Aggregate Score	Prizes
1	W. H. Jackson	220	1st	70 68 68 206 $1.07	74 71 68 213 $2.71	73 69 72 214 $.50	633	$100 $50 G.C. Rifle
2	J. S. Sumner	251	1st	72 71 66 209 1.07	72 66 72 210 1.07	71 65 74 210 15.	629	none
3	Frank Hyde	219	1st	71 71 62 204 1.07	71 71 69 211 1.57	72 67 72 211 25.	626	none
4	S. I. Scott	214	1st	72 71 67 210 5.07	71 66 70 207 .71	70 69 69 208 10.	625	Rem. C Rifle
5	J. F. Brown	215	1st	74 66 64 204 1.07	72 73 68 213 5.07	74 68 66 208	625	none
6	K. K. Furrow	209	2d	71 71 67 209 2.607	73 66 70 209 .71	66 66 65 197	615	100. and Bal. C. Rifle
7	R. Rathbone	209	2d	71 69 65 205 1.07	69 65 67 201 .71	68 66 72 206	612	25.
8	N. Washburn	213	1st	72 69 67 208 11.07	69 65 72 206 .71	72 67 59 198	612	none
9	W. Gerrish	218	1st	70 71 62 203 1.07	70 66 70 206 .71	66 64 72 202	611	none
10	E. H. Sanford	207	2d	73 66 65 204 1.07	71 60 70 201 .71	67 61 73 201	606	15.
11	J. L. Allen	213	1st	72 68 62 202 1.07	63 68 65 196	74 66 68 208	606	none
12	C. H. Laird	210	2d	72 66 62 200 1.07	69 70 65 204 .71	65 70 67 202	606	none
13	K. K. DeForest	185	4th	70 71 61 202 1.07	69 67 67 203 .71	70 65 64 199	604	$50. Badge
14	E. E. Pray	no record	4th	65 64 65 194	66 71 64 201	70 72 68 208	603	25
15	J. W. Parks	187	4th	72 71 63 206 1.07	67 64 67 198	72 58 65 195	599	15.
16	J. P. Waters	207	2d	66 66 62 194	68 69 62 199	66 62 69 197	590	none
17	C. A. Perry	196	4th	65 61 62 188	73 69 66 208 .71	64 64 64 192	588	none
18	H. Fisher Jr	204	3d	71 64 55 190	70 63 67 200	72 67 54 193	583	50.
19	J. H. Gray	204	3d	65 63 52 180	72 62 65 199	72 63 59 194	573	25.
20	G. L. Morse	207	2d	64 63 57 184	64 68 68 200	64 54 64 182	566	none
21	S. Wilder	210	2d	63 66 46 175	70 66 68 204 .71	71 54 56 181	560	none
22	J. W. Shurter	no record	4th	70 63 64 197	69 66 65 200	51 58 48 157	554	Five Papers one year and thru Perry's Book
23	W. Poland	207	2d	68 67 60 195	68 63 64 195	66 40 R		
24	S. I. G. Dudley	203	3d	70 63 50 183	69 65 66 200	72 R		
25	H. S. Rockwell	211	2d	71 67 59 196	61 R.	70 62 R		
26	A. A. Adee	197	4th	61 68 61 190	59 65 61 185	a		
27	F. Wessel	208	3d	68 64 56 188	67 D			
28	W. Parker	202	3d	65 62 53 180	67 57 65 189	a		
29	E. Reader	200	4th	66 52 44 162	58 65 65 188	a		
30	G. F. Ferris	195	4th	48 50 62 160	66 66 67 199	a		Total Prizes
31	L. L. Hepburn	204	3d	64 65 R	63 67 65 195	a		$1219.
32	J. A. Hatry	191	4th	55 57 R	a	a		
33	J. Tully	no record	4th	59 44 13 116	44 45 54 143	48 48 R		
34	R. H. Keene	207	2d			64 R		

$50. offered for score in excess of 219 points not won
$15. offered for 3d prize 3d class not won only two completed scores in 3d class.

Abbreviations {R: retired a: absent D: Disqualified}

Long-range Tournament shot at Creedmoor Sept. 22, 23 and 24. 1879

No	Rifle	Shell	Powder				Bullet				Wad	Loaded from	Remarks
			grains	maker	wt.	meas.	gr.	hardens	Style	make			
1	S.C.B.	U.M.C.	106	L&R	6	Weigh	550	1/14	L.P.H.B.	U.M.C.	2 thin	Breech	Miss 1000 Yds. 1st & 2d day. Cost $50. & $25.
2	do	do	110	"	5	do	"	"	"	"	"	do	Bull on wrong target 9 o'c'ks 2d day Cost $300.
3	do	do	109	"	"	do	"	"	"	"	"	do	do do do 3d day Oct. $26.
4	R.C.	Rem	115	Haz Fg	"	Meas	"	1/10	L.P. Hep	Rem	none	Muzzle	Miss 900 Yds 2d day Bullet too light Cost $15.
5	S.C.B.	U.M.C.	110	L&R	"	Weigh	"	1/14	L.P.H.B.	U.M.C.	1, thin	Breech	
6	B.d.	Bd.Conductr	115	"	6	Meas	"	1/11	L.P. Bd.	Winch	none	Muzzle	Miss 800 Yds 3d day Unaccountable
7	S.C.B.	U.M.C.	110	"	5	Weigh	"	"	L.P.H.B.	Winch	"	do	Sick, Miss 900 Yds. 3d day Bullet bad Cost $125.
8	do	do	106	"	"	do	"	1/14	"	U.M.C.	1, thin	Breech	
9	do	do	105	"	5	do	"	"	"	"	"	do	Miss 800 Yds 3d day Unaccountable
10	SC.cl.	do	105	Haz Fg	"	do	"	1/11	"	Winch	none	Muzzle	2d day Bull on wrong target 800 Yds
11	S.C.B.	do 23/4 215	107 103	"	"	Miss. Weigh	"	1/14	"	U.M.C.	1, thin	Breech	3d - 1st shot 1000 Yds miss cause of Elevation
12	R.C.	Rem	110	"	"	do	"	1/11	L.P. Hep	Rem	none	Muzzle	Miss 1000 Yds 3d day 36 inch barrel Miss at 1000 Yds.
13	do	do	103½	"	"	do	"	"	"	"	"	Breech	on 1st & 2d days. Burst Shells.
14	SCB	U.M.C.	105	"	"	Flask	"	1/14	L.P.H.B.	U.M.C.	"	Muzzle	Never fired a shot before August
15	R.C.	Rem	97	"	"	Weigh	"	1/11	L.P. Hep	Rem	1, thin	Breech	
16	S.C.B.	U.M.C.	105	L&R	"	do	"	1/14	L.P.H.B.	U.M.C.	"	do	
17	do	Winch	110	"	6	Meas	"	1/11	"	Winch	none	Muzzle	Last day caps would not explode
18	S.C.cl.	do	102	"	"	Weigh	"	"	"	"	1, thin	Breech	
19	R.C.	Rem	103	Haz Fg	"	do	"	"	L.P. Hep	Rem	"	do	
20	Cc.cl.	U.M.C.	105	L&R	"	Meas	"	"	L.P.	U.M.C.	none	Muzzle	
21	S.C.B.	do	110	"	"	Weigh	"	"	Hall		1, thin	Breech	1st day no glass to shot his shots with
22	R.C.	Winch	100	Haz Fg	"	do	"	1/11	L.P. Hep	Winch	none	do	3d day. Shells old continually bursting
23	do	Rem	104	Lith	"	do	"	"	"	Rem	1, thin	do	
24	SCB	U.M.C.	103	Haz Fg	"	do	"	1/14	L.P.H.B.	U.M.C.	none	Muzzle	Could easily have won 1st prize 3d class but for retiring
25	R.C.	Rem	116 107	L&R	5	do	"	1/11	L.P. Hep	Rem	1, thin	Breech	Not in practice
26	do	do	111½	Haz Fg	"	Meas	"	"	"	"	none	Muzzle	Old Shells bursting
27	do	do	106	"	"	Weigh	"	"	"	Winch	1, thin	Breech	Accidental discharge of piece owing trigger pull, Disqualified
28	do	do	105	"	"	do	"	"	"	"	"	Muzzle	Untested bullets, too loose.

LONG RANGE TOURNAMENT—BY CLASSES.

1ST CLASS, WITH A RECORD OF BETTER THAN 212 POINTS.

	Loaded at	1st day.	2d day.	3d day.	Total.	Total prizes.
1. Jackson	Breech	206	213	214	633	$336 78
2. Sumner	Breech	209	210	210	629	41 78
3. Hyde	Breech	2 4	211	211	626	41 78
4. Scott	Muzzle	210	207	208	625	169 78
5. Brown	Breech	204	213	208	625	51 78
8. Washburn	Breech	208	206	198	612	11 78
9. Gerrish	Breech	203	206	202	611	1 78
11. Allen (last day)	Breech	202	196	208	606	1 07

2D CLASS, WITH A RECORD OF FROM 206 TO 212 POINTS.

	Loaded at	1st day.	2d day.	2d day.	Total.	Total prizes.
6. Farrow	Muzzle	209	209	197	615	$226 78
7. Rathbone	Muzzle	205	201	206	612	26 78
10. Sanford	Muzzle	204	201	201	606	16 78
12. Laird	Muzzle	200	204	202	606	0 71
16. Waters	Breech	194	199	197	590	......
20. Morse	Muzzle	184	200	182	566	......
21. Wilder	Breech	175	204	181	560	0 71
23. Poland	Breech	195	195	R.	Ret.	......
25. Rockwell	Breech	196	R.	R.	Ret.	......
34. Keene	Muzzle	...	...	R.	Ret.	......

3D CLASS, WITH A RECORD OF FROM 200 TO 206 POINTS.

	Loaded at	1st day.	2d day.	3d day.	Total.	Total prizes.
18. Fisher	Breech	190	200	193	583	$50 00
19. Gray	Breech	180	199	194	573	25 00
24. Dudley	Muzzle	188	200	R.	Ret.	......
27. Wessel	Breech	188	D.	...	D.	......
28. Parker	Muzzle	180	189	A.	Ret.	......
31. Hepburn	Breech	R.	195	A.	Ret.	......

4TH CLASS, WITHOUT A RECORD OF 200 POINTS.

	Loaded at	1st day.	2d day.	3d day.	Total.	Total prizes.
13. De Forest	Breech	202	203	199	604	$51 78
14. Pray	Muzzle	194	201	208	603	25 00
15. Partis	Breech	206	198	195	599	16 07
17. Perry	Muzzle	188	208	192	588	0 71
22. Shurter	Breech	197	200	157	554 (Low)	14 00
26. Adee	Muzzle	190	185	A.	Ret.	......
29. Reader	Breech	163	188	A.	Ret.	......
30. Ferris	Muzzle	160	199	A.	Ret.	......
32. Hatry	Breech	117 R.	A.	A.	Ret.	......
33. Tully	Muzzle	116	143	96 R.	Ret.	......

Note.—Jackson won the Sharps' Standard Long-range Rifle, and the Laflin and Rand powder prize.

Scott won the Remington Creedmoor Rifle.

Farrow won the Ballard Long-range Rifle.

Shurter made the most "inners," the most "centers," and the lowest score of 135 shots.

Third prize, 3d class, not won; and prize for first completed score in excess of 219 points, not won.

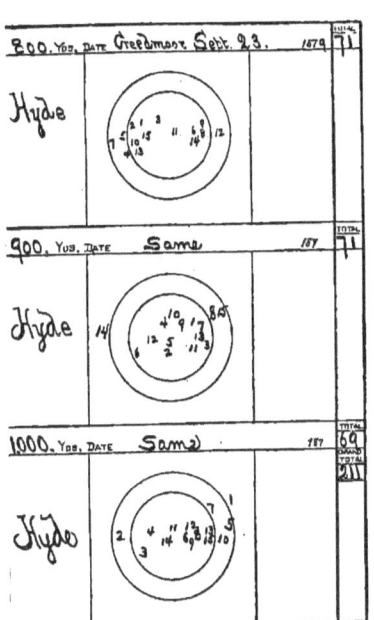
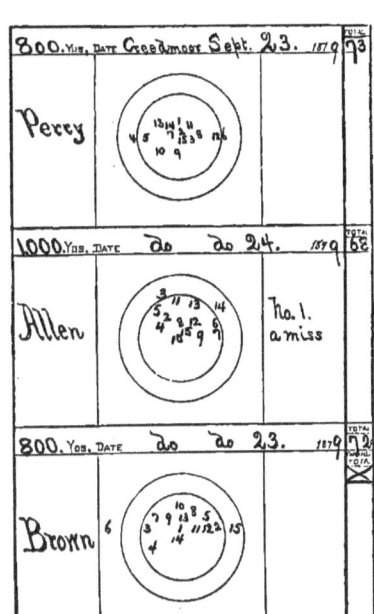

Selected Scores Long-range Tournament

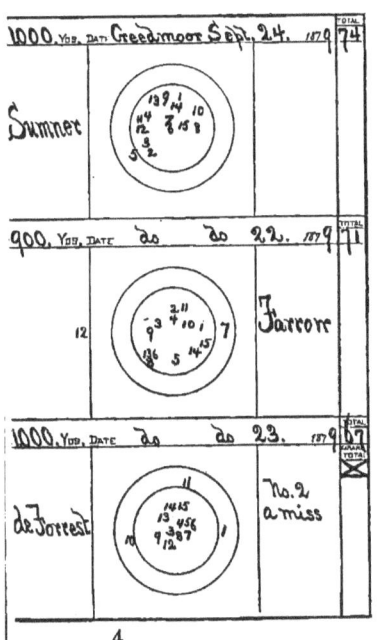
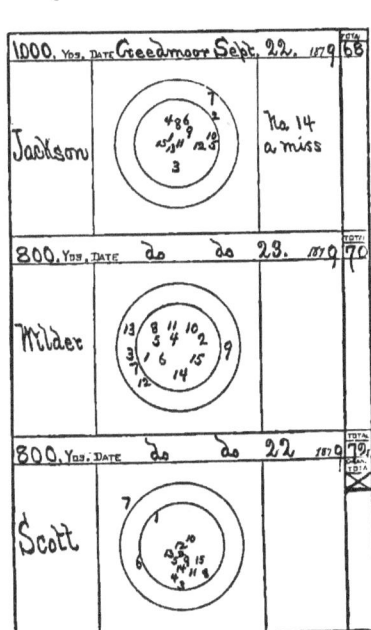

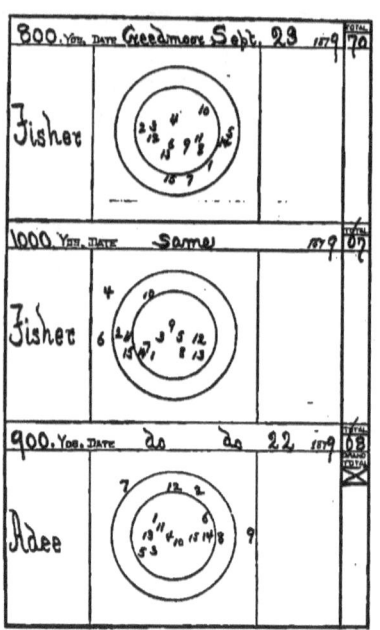
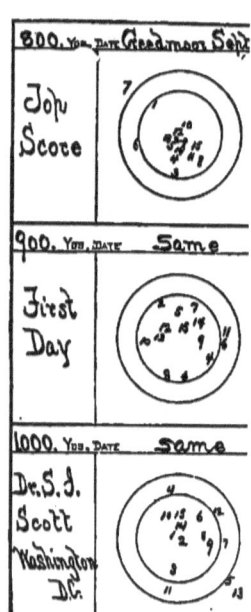

Selected Scores Long-range Tournament

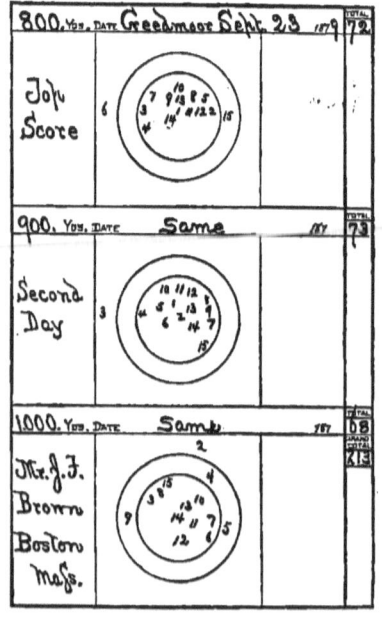
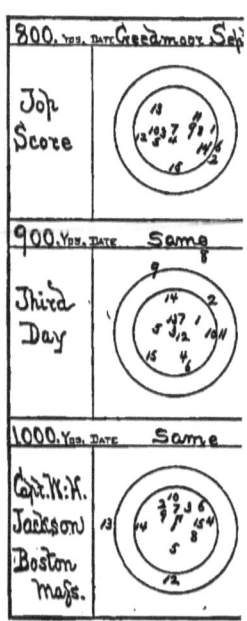

MODERN OBSERVATIONS ON RIFLE SHOOTING.

The author believes that, with a complete set of fine instruments for indicating the elements, and with Anemometers stationed at intervals of one hundred yards down the range and a certain distance toward the direction from which the wind comes, it is within the possibility of man to place consecutive shots on the same perpendicular line for windage. This state of affairs is impossible in warfare, and, in fact, undesirable in peace, for then nothing would be left to the shooter either in judgment or luck, and fine rifle shooting would no longer be an enjoyable pastime. The application of science is necessary, in so far as it can secure to all a certainty of putting all the shots on a given horizontal line when elements and other things are equal.

If a shooter is fairly certain that all his shots will be right as to elevation, in his battle with the wind and other elements, he will have the advantage of a clearer judgment, and mark the results of such confidence on the target. This article, then, will treat on elevations, and the very many details necessary to produce the greatest uniformity in that regard. In order to cover all the points, let us begin on page 14 of Modern Observations and follow the headings: RIFLES.—We find the two muzzle-loaders at the foot of the list in the hands of Ferris and Tully. SIGHTS.—We again find Capt. Tully, with the Goodwin bar, at the foot of the list, while all of the best scores were made with the open bead. SHELLS.—Jackson had a miss at 1,000 yards on the first and second days, and lost top place on both days thereby. He says:

"I attribute my misses to moisture collecting under the reinforce of the shells and imparting that moisture to the powder. I now rebake my shells just before loading."

De Forest, top man of the 4th Class, says:

"As requested, I herewith send you my best targets on elevation, but don't advise you to make any *accurate* deductions from them. Both misses were caused by shells bursting, and five other low shots at the shorter distances were the results of a like misfortune."

With a straight shell, a close chamber and an action that does not spring, bursting shells do not injure the shooting to so great a degree, but if the shell bursts so as to permit the burning gas to escape rearwards, the effect must be disastrous. The result is multiplied the nearer you approach the capacity of the rifle to burn the quantity of powder you use. If you use a much greater quantity of powder than the rifle will burn, the loss of gas will not be as material.

Several others had similar ill luck. On the last day Shurter was thoroughly broken up from bursting shells, and was absolutely unable to rely on a shot in making his estimation for the next. Let us take warning now, and forever, by these examples. If your means call for such economy as the use of shells until they burst, is it prudent to shoot so much? It is the experience of a great many that a shell should be shot once in practice and then kept for a match, to be discarded when used the second time. If you are sure they will last longer, take the responsibility, and pocket the results without a murmur. POWDER.—Please consult the table on this topic. The quantity to be used depends on other considerations, and will be treated on in connection with bullet, loading, &c. It is the author's belief that the difference in average elevation between L. & R., Nos. 5 and 6, is partly due to their relative density and in favor of No. 6. No. 5 occupies less space for a given number of grains. BULLETS.—It is remarkable with what unanimity the 550-grain bullet has been adopted; also its shape, long point. The papering is the same, except that in the Hepburn style the paper is gathered in at the base, while in the Hyde base pattern the paper is gathered in and then cut out, making it easier for the bullet to strip.

The author desires to call attention to an error which doubtless accounts in no small degree for the misfortune of one of the shooters in the Tournament. In a letter he stated that he had been giving his attention to comparative size of bullets. In order to classify them he had taken the Hyde Base Bullets and pushed them into the muzzle of his rifle; the result was that he loosened the patches unevenly. Another says:

"The 14th shot missed on account of being too tight, and as I was muzzle-loading it pushed the bullet nearly through the patch, which prevented the patch from being cut off of the bullet, and, of course, the consequence was a miss."

There is likely to be a revolution in bullets this year, as several practical riflemen are producing new styles and weights. This will partially involve an alteration in quantity of powder and length of shell if used in fixed ammunition. The test of quantity of powder to be used should be as before; find how much the bullet makes the gun burn and then use a few grains more. If muzzle-loading, use more than the shell will hold and the rifle burn. WADS.—The wads used as expressed in the tables are virtually equivalent to no wad; made of writing paper or thin card-board, they only serve to hold the powder in the shell, peradventure the bullet (being lightly seated) should drop out. The term "no wads" (on page 18) has reference to lubricated wads, or anything like them that serve as an elastic cushion to deaden the initial blow necessary to properly upset the bullet. LOADING AMMUNITION.—Much must be said on this topic. Simply to state how it should be done, ought to suffice, but does not seem to. Of course this refers to fixed ammunition. * Some muzzle-load from necessity, and some to secure better elevations. Making rules so exact as the author has, it would seem that he would follow them, but having lost his right arm it is hard work for him to make fixed ammunition, and this was his reason for loading at the muzzle, and the kink of using more powder than the shell would hold, was simply invented to avoid having to re-shape the mouth of the shells. All other things being equal, this kind of loading will produce the best elevations (see Perry's target among selected scores). The author made a target at 1,000 yards, at Brinton Range, in 1878, in a match where not more than six inches of the target were used for elevation by the fifteen shots. There are other considerations that must be included. Hyde's targets for elevation are more eloquent than volumes in favor of proper, fixed ammunition, and the article on page 20 explains how he makes it. Follow it implicitly. If you have no tube long enough, pour the powder slowly through the barrel of your rifle. The shooter who has the best long-range average in the world once said to the author: "From the first I bought what your book called for in OUTFIT FOR LONG RANGE, and have always followed your advice in loading and everything else, just as laid down in your book, and if you would do the same thing you would shoot better than you do." The table will show the large number who use fixed ammunition, and a careful note of Allen's third day in comparison with the first and second, together with his own words, will give the author's judgment also: "I think I am converted to fixed ammunition, not because it shoots better, but because it gives you more time to watch the results of others' shooting, and discover in this way changes in wind and elevation that would not have been detected otherwise."

In addition to the misfortune of pushing the bullet through the patch when muzzle-loading (liable to occur without your knowing it), there are other mishaps very possible, such as putting in the powder having forgotten to put in a shell, thus losing a charge of powder, and causing you to have to stop and clean out again, forgetting to put in a bullet, leaving the rod in on top of the bullet, etc., etc. Very many riflemen, in order to make time, so that a day can be spared from business, do so at the expense of loading properly; they take good care to be in condition on the day of the shooting, but how about their condition when loading? Patience is a most important ingredient in making ammunition, and when a shooter sits down to make his cartridges, he should be the opposite of a tired, sleepy man. He should have time to spare, and should preclude the possibility of interruption. He should have enough shells that have been fired an equal number of times. He should know that EACH ONE is perfect in every particular. He should take nothing for granted. Absolute test of everything is the only safeguard against what you may claim is an "unaccountable" miss, one of which ruins a score. CLEANING.—One of the shooters says: "The greatest trouble I have ever had is about elevations, and that I take it is a 'gun' peculiarity. While some guns will hold their elevations perfectly for fifteen shots, another will be increasing or reducing elevations. Another day and these same guns may reverse their characteristics. I have often said that when a man has a gun that will hold elevations, he has no excuse for a low score." Is it possible that one rifle will act differently from another under similar treatment? Certainly not. Then there is a reason for trouble. The eye has something to do with it, also heat and cold, air pressure, force of wind, &c., but the fact that the gun works oppositely on different days, and especially when other rifles are holding elevations, proves the rule. One day is moist, the other dry. The author has taken rifles pronounced clean, they looked clean, very bright, a dry rag was put through to prove it; the author put through patch after patch, wet, and brought them out fouled. The very best shooters fail to get their rifles clean, and this is why they creep up and then jump down, and *vice versa*. On the 23d, at 800 yards, at the same target, with a comparatively dry atmosphere, one of our best shooters (making 74 points), increased his elevation 1¾ points; Perry increased ½ point on the 11th shot only. At 800 yards, on the 24th, from the time the Hygrometer registered close to 100 per-centum of moisture, he made no alteration; Perry made none from the first shot— fine scores of exceptional shots, have been watched carefully, and compared shot for shot by the author, *and he believes what he says*. When the air is dry, the powder soon gathers on the inside of the barrel, and polishes so as to look like the barrel; dry rags, with friction however great, do not remove it. Water or oil alone will. The author has tried one set of patches through forty-five shots; the first fifteen were excellent for elevation, the last fifteen were not. Read articles on pages 26 to 31 carefully. AIMING AND FIRING.—Quite a number have owned up to indifferent holding. The following being the best sample for beginners to become familiar with, is printed for their benefit: "Let me make honest confession between ourselves. Mishap No. 1—A low four for first shot at 800 yards; cause, a careless pull off, and I know it, too, for don't you see I don't alter my elevation for the next, or for the six succeeding shots. The 5th a center, was for not paying attention to wind. The 7th and 15th, want of good holding. Now, nothing but my own carelessness prevented a full score. 900 yards, shot No. 1—A deliberate pull off, with both eyes shut, probably. You will observe on this target that there was a lack of nerve in not putting elevation down, and too much nerve in screwing that wind gauge. The 1,000 yards target shows fewer mistakes than the others. Now, Captain, I think you will say enough, but perhaps it may be somewhat refreshing to have an honest excuse given for a bad score [200 points]; it certainly seems to give some relief to yours truly."

WEATHER.—Perhaps no match has ever been fired wherein so many changes in weather had to be overcome. On the morning of the first day the air was cold and raw; everything seemed to threaten the immediate approach of the line storm. The wind came from the N. E., changing considerably in force and direction. Many of the riflemen failed to appear, and the match was not called until 11 o'clock. The only genial smile that came from old Sol appeared after the close of the 1,000 yards shooting. On the second day everything appeared delightful. The thermometer indicated 70°, and the light was fair, MIRAGE alone interfering. The wind came from the S. W., and remained fairly steady all day. On the third day the wind came at the start from the S. W., gradually working up to W., when a perfect gale and storm came up. This passed over, leaving the wind coming from the N.W., and the elevations no one seemed to know where. The range was 900 yards.

Allen went up 2+2+2=6 points before getting right. Jackson went up 8½ points, afterward reducing 1½ points. Sumner went up 5 points. Perry, 3½ +1=4½ points. Wilder went up 4½, afterwards reducing 1 point, while Brown went up 1+1=2 points. At the close of the 900 yards' shooting another heavy storm drove the riflemen under cover. After severe rain for forty minutes the sun broke forth in all his glory, the wind coming from the west. This bright light occasioned considerable mirage, and put the shooters to their trumps to find the target again. The differences in elevations recorded above are not only remarkable but present a problem, which, the more it is considered, seems the more to require scientific study. The difference on account of direction of wind would seem to be more than Brown made, and the possibility of mistake suggested itself, but on reviewing the scores, it was found that all shot through at 900 yards without further change, and nothing remarkable occurred until they went to the 1,000 yards range, with a change in light, from clouds to bright sun and mirage. Jackson, Sumner and Wilder went up the usual 24 points, Allen and Perry 23½, while Brown went up an unusual 26 points, all making splendid shooting. The author was about to leave this subject thus, "Some day it will be understood why Jackson required 7, Allen 6, Sumner 5, Perry 4½, Wilder 3½, and Brown but 2 points more in elevation," but as the rifles and ammunition were *equivalent* (absolutely), their positions the same, viz.: shooting from the arm-pit, sight on the heel of the butt, 100 per centum of moisture, thermometer and barometer holding steady, wind direction and force equal for all, the author concluded to try and solve the problem. He went to Boston and met the shooters with their score books. The details were full and correct as had been reported. Jackson actually required his 7 points, and Brown only required his 2 points. If either had read his Vernier wrong then Allen stood there requiring 6 points, while Wilder required but 3½ points.

The actual mathematical calculation of difference, 6¾ in. to a point counting from Brown's hit, would have thrown Jackson over the target, but the actual deviation at 900 yards for a point is greater. The author knows of no shooter who having a central bulls-eye would like to risk putting his elevation up a point, if he wished to stay in the "bull."

After a consultation of two hours it was concluded that the difference must be located in the EYE. Allen has a light grey, Sumner a grey, Wilder a grey, Jackson a light hazel, Perry a hazel, and Brown a dark hazel eye. Jackson's eye is darker, but Jackson and Brown both have the same range and kind of vision, both using the same kind of glasses for near vision, while either can read a newspaper 6 feet away with the unassisted eye. Sumner's vision is clear at all distances. Allen's is exceptionally so, while Perry and Wilder require glasses to shoot with, being unable to define at a distance. Perry has a perfect vision within two feet distance, while Wilder uses glasses for all distances. The difference in the size of the peep-holes in the sight cups doubtless contributes to the complication. The pressure being made for the immediate production of this book, together with the fact that the season of the year is unpropitious for experimental study of these phenomena, forbids further research for treatment in this edition.

The author desires that any discrepancy of the kind that may occur in future shall be sent to him, with all the data the score diagrams call for minutely given, also the color of the eyes and a statement as to the power of vision of the different eyes, size of peep-holes, amount of metal in front and behind the hole, and if the hole is beveled from front or rear, or both, etc.

In thus following the detail as laid down in the book, the treatment may seem to be disconnected. Do not throw this paper aside because it may appear uninteresting. Do not read it lightly either. The highest encomiums the author has had came from those who had come to study "Modern Observations" as a text book, and then, after they had become most proficient in shooting.

Rifle shooting is a science of which simply burning powder and using lead as projectiles are the A B C's. However dry or however insurmountable the rules and obstacles may appear, face them with as much persistency as you would face a profession or a trade. Rifle shooting is nothing else in the abstract, but the fact that it is a costly amusement, thus making indulgence in it select, probably, is the reason why so many amateurs, taking it up, reduce it to a pastime instead of a profession. In proportion as it is costly, in just that proportion ought its votaries to approach it with all the knowledge attainable. We might as well expect that novices should shut the doors of their senses against the inventions of the telephone and electric light, and still plod on in search of such inventions, as to expect a recruit in rifle shooting to ignore rules so carefully worked out in that science.

In concluding this article the author would recommend the use of a center fire straight shell (so called), made of hard brass, holding ten grains more powder than the rifle will burn, allowing the bullet to be barely seated, marking the shell before using, so that it can be inserted in the chamber the same way each time it is used. Secure an instrument for resizing the mouths of the shells. Select your powder after consulting the table. If you get a keg, secure also 1-lb. cans, and after seeing that they are very clean and dry, pour from the keg into the cans, and then seal the cans till used. If you use it out of the keg as needed, you will fail to get results from the last loading equal to the first. The author uses a Wilkinson loader to measure charges of powder, and gets great evenness by putting the powder in a Curtis's & Harvey's powder can, and, placing the finger over the mouth of the can, inverting it in the funnel of the loader. The shoulders of the can take off the pressure of the powder, and thus the loader produces the same weight each time.

The first three or four charges should be discarded, until the loader gets fairly in operation. For fear of accident in the loader, the author weighs in addition, unless specially pressed for time, which, by the way, he don't allow to be the case. For Bullets, consult the table and the new styles. Use a thin wad, like Bristol card, in loading the shells with powder, just to keep the powder from spilling out. As Allen says, "When you load at the breech, you have more time to watch the elements and the shooting of others." If you will load at the muzzle, do not use Hyde Base bullets, as the act of pushing them through the barrel will (perhaps once in a hundred times) loosen the paper.

The author finds no reason to change the articles on pages 26 to 31, and believes that they give advice which can only be modified in isolated individual cases. SPOTTING THE SHOTS and KEEPING SCORE.—One competitor says: "My targets in the Tournament are poor and, therefore, not worth preserving." Do not fall into this error; preserve the record of every shot, and accurately describe the reason of the failure to the best of your ability. If every shot was thrown on the target perfectly, you would keep it to look at; very good. The elements might have been perfect for shooting, and it teaches nothing; but if you have a poor target there must be a reason for it, and if you record that reason, you will be the better able to avoid like failure again.

Another competitor says: "I never have been accustomed to spot my shots with a glass. Had I been bright enough to have availed myself of such helps as others in my vicinity used, perhaps the showing might have been more favorable."

Still another says: "I am sorry that I cannot give you any information with regard to my shooting in the Tournament at Creedmoor, as I did not keep any diagram or record on that occasion."

One competitor made a miss that he could have avoided: "I would not have fired the shot if I had not been behind, from having several miss-fires previous. My companions on the target were complaining of my keeping them waiting."

This gentleman could have passed his turn and reloaded, saving his miss, taking third place and $15, also making his aggregate score second only to Jackson's. *Such complaining ends when the score is done,* and to-day he would be lauded by those who then complained if he had scored a bull's-eye instead of a miss. Page 36 is fully endorsed by the column of remarks in the tables. Study the errors or mishaps and their cost. Come to an understanding like this: "I can nearly always trace my misses to some avoidable cause; in other words, they are nearly all from carelessness." And if you do get a miss, find out why, if it costs days of thought, in the interests of the science and your brother riflemen.

LONG-RANGE, WITH MILITARY RIFLES.

☞ HOLD YOUR RIFLE PLUMB. ☜

In writing an article under this heading, the author is constrained to reproduce "An Open Letter on Military Sights," which explains itself. The letter was to have been replied to openly, but the only answer as yet published has appeared in the concessions made by General Wingate in the use of military rifles in the National Guard, State of New York, and in the changed rules of the National Rifle Association.

By way of further preface to the article, the author desires to say that the changes are not radical enough, and that the improvement will have to eventually come to perfection. It remains for some officer in authority to grasp the occasion, and thus earn the right to be referred to in years to come as *having given so much* towards perfecting the military rifle.

AN OPEN LETTER ON MILITARY SIGHTS.

(From *The National Guardsman*, June 1, 1878.)

The following letter from Captain E. A. Perry to the General Inspector of Rifle Practice speaks for itself :

NEW YORK, May 8, 1878.

Colonel GEO. W. WINGATE,
General Inspector of Rifle Practice, N. G. S. N. Y.:

COLONEL—In addressing you on the subject of military sights I not only recognize the fact that you are the responsible authority of the Empire State, empowered to make alterations if deemed advisable, but you are a Director of the National Rifle Association, chiefly consulted in such matters; you are the author of a Manual on military rifle shooting, generally adopted by the different State Governments and portions of the Army and Navy; you are, in the words of many besides myself, "the father of rifle shooting in this country."

Believing that you are ever ready to adopt improvements when the theory and experience of others demonstrate that change can be made for the better, I presume to call your attention to conclusions which I have arrived at after careful practice and study.

I do not assume to be the inventor of any ideas that I may advance, nor will I claim originality other than this, application of many methods for the production of a general and, as I deem, a much needed result.

Long-range matches with military rifles being introduced, required of me that I should add suggestions to my treatise in "Perry's Green Book," and in my practice I have had the crudity of military sights and their inaptitude for fine work forced on my attention.

My earnestness has been aroused from the fact that I found rifle manufacturers willing to improve military sights, but just as improvement was made necessary by the introduction of long-range matches, the National Rifle Association changed its interpretation of a military rifle in the Regulations for the present year, fairly prohibiting the changes that the manufacturers would willingly make. This restriction was, I understand, copied from the regulations of the N. R. A. of Great Britain; it is to be hoped unwittingly. Whatever may be concluded as best by our mother country (perhaps unwittingly also), Uncle Sam is cute enough to devise something a little more advantageous.

In pursuing my inquiries among manufacturers, the manager for one of our principal rifle companies used the remark—"For the last twenty years we have done all we could to improve military rifles, but have never done anything to improve the sights." How many years back the rear-sight leaf was scaled for elevations I am at a loss to determine. Of course improvement in rifling, in powder, in bullets, cartridges, etc., etc., during all these years, has flattened the trajectory, but the figures 1, 2, etc., have been stamped on the rear sight, constantly, in the good old way, until, if you should set the sight now for 1,000 yards, and fire an improved cartridge, the ball would pass at least 75 feet over the object aimed at. The more I have pursued this theme, the more I have become convinced that in our late war nine-tenths of all the shots fired, with the sights regulated for a prescribed distance, went far beyond the mark, and the place of greatest safety was the line aimed at.

My first suggestion is that the sights be scaled short of the distance, so, if the object is not hit direct, the chances are two to one in favor of a *ricochet*, which would prove dangerous, and show what more elevation would be required. This would always be the safe side, even for erroneous judgments of distances. The *one* caution on the battle-field was "fire low." Many, many thousands of times have I heard it. It need never have been uttered had the elevations been marked low. Elevation is the only essential feature when a "line of battle" is the object; right and left shots have ample field for destructive work. The remark has often been made at Creedmoor, when the military teams have been shooting, "What an awful skirmish line that would make." How true in comparison to our skirmish lines in action; but, passing down that line, not one rifle could be found with the sights regulated as scaled, and with but very few with the same sighting right and left. Some would be aiming on the target, others off. Intelligence produced the results, but if the sights had been right that intelligence could have been employed for still better results.

The fact that sight taken across the straight edge of the sliding bar (rather than through the V) gives better elevations, has been recognized by yourself, and also through you by the N. R. A. The natural perverseness of human nature, or some other cause, prevents many from taking a sufficiently small portion of the front sight to enable them to hold all the advantages of the straight bar, and so I have been induced to seek a more certain restriction for accuracy.

At the long ranges even great care is not sufficient to properly gauge the amount of front sight showing above the flat bar. The most natural substitute, and one which has been tried by Colonel Bodine with success, one also which is adopted on the Remington sporting rifle, but more especially on the Peabody-Martini Kill-Deer rifle, was the peep-hole. Three peep-holes, made an eighth of an inch apart, right and left, and about a sixteenth from the top, admit of taking a sight for elevation each time alike; the whole of the front sight showing, the point of it can be located at a given point on the target with certainty, and for successive shots with known uniformity. The peep-hole admits of seeing all that is passing in front, the appearance of the hole when the eye is looking through it (not at it), being very much like a V, the metal above it serving to mark the hole, but not offering a sufficient barrier to the necessary vision of what may be transpiring in front while the aim is being taken. Three holes are suggested. On a still day, the rifle being centered, the middle hole, being in the center of the sliding bar, can be used, and the *point aimed at* varied; for a right wind the right hole can be used, etc. The *two* holes not in use can readily be stopped with dirt or straw. In this way, with but little ingenuity, at whatever distance and in whatever wind, the object to be hit can always be aimed at, or approximately aimed at.

So far I have not suggested anything that calls for new sights or new mechanical device. I would have the sights scaled just short of actual elevations, and the distances between the figures, from 2 to 3 or 9 to 10, divided into tenths, so that a record could be kept of elevations. This and the three peep-holes could be added at an insignificant cost.

A Vernier screw is not necessary; in fact I think it would be detrimental; the distance for the sliding bar to move is small, as the sights are so near together.

I feel somewhat confident that you will agree with me on the foregoing, but I wish to go further and suggest sights in comparison with the excellent shooting qualities of all the military arms made. Why have a rifle made that will shoot accurately, and then employ means of sighting it, that, to produce results, require the skill of a surveyor? Why not have sights that in themselves contain the skill? To accomplish so much but little is necessary. The sliding bar, with its three peep-holes, is good enough, but the rear sight could, without detriment to any interest, be carried back a little nearer the eye, say to the "breech pin." The leaf could hinge on a screw, which could move the sight right and left; not much, for we have three peep-holes; an eighth of an inch play is enough. The sight would be stronger than it is now, as the pin of the hinge is but one-tenth of an inch in diameter, and the screw which would take its place would have to be much larger.

In "line-of-battle" firing the wind gauge, subdivisions of elevation and peep-holes might not be necessary. When that time arrives the V, straight edge of the sliding bar, and the front sights are undisturbed. In skirmishing, for annoying batteries, picking off pickets, and all such more skillful uses, my suggestions increase the capacity for accuracy three hundred per cent. over the present sights. I have tried them, and believe in them, and I think I can demonstrate them to others in actual practice.

I have the honor to be, very respectfully, your obedient servant,

EDWIN A. PERRY.

The concession in relation to sights is no less a matter of congratulation than is the permission to use any position for distances above 300 yards. It now remains for the authorities to allow the peep-hole and carry the sight back nearer the eye, especially if the back position is adopted by the riflemen.

The author has "conjured up" a back sight suitable for rifles, with a metal breech frame, which is far stronger than those now in use, and which *does not required to be centered* before it can be closed, viz., an arch frame straddling the breech frame, beveled in, and having on the top of the arch a suitable peep-hole, traveling by transverse screw adjustment, in a beveled frame, which protects the screw and offers windage the full width of the breech frame. A similar traveling peep-hole could be put on a sight to be inserted in the heel of the butt of the rifle, to be removed when not in use by pulling it out. It would have to fit close to avoid lost motion. Its length would be determined by the drop of the butt stock. Elevation in both cases at the breech frame or butt, would be gauged by lowering or raising the sight, the peep-hole apparatus being above and entirely free from interference by or with elevations.

In all this gain, the bayonet stud has not been interfered with. The beauty of the peep-hole, though acting more as a V, is, that once you look through it (and you will know if you do not), your only effort is to put the point of the bayonet stud wherever you please on the target. There is no longer any speculation as to how much front sight you are using, and you will be all the more liable to think to hold your rifle plumb. When you are shooting in the back position, you can readily see if the rifle is plumb.

There are several ways to sight over a straight edge back sight. The author takes the least bit of the tip of the front sight, and aims along the top edge of the target, cutting the target into imaginary points of windage, and relieving the eye of the glare of the full target. Others take in the whole tip of the front sight down to the bayonet stud, aiming along the top of the target with the tip of the front sight.

Others use the V in the rear sight, taking so much of the front sight as will touch a line drawn across the top of the V. Some one of the above plans should be settled on, and adhered to, so that the sighting becomes a habit. Practice at home. Capt. Jackson spends one or two hours each day, except Sundays, sighting his rifles at home.

Position is the next important feature. On pages 22 and 24 this subject is treated in all earnestness. The author desires, right here, to say that when men are taken to the mid-range firing points they are allowed to throw themselves into erroneous positions, either through the ignorance or criminal indifference of the instructor or the egotism so common to beginners. *In long-range shooting in the prone position* the instructions on page 24 MUST be followed in order to obtain even fair results.

The article on **Wind** on page 28 should be learned; as also **Allowance**, etc., on page 32. As the sights on military rifles are nearer to each other than on fine rifles with the Vernier on the grip, less change would be needed to produce a given result. Sight taken across a line drawn on the sliding bar 1-32 of an inch to the right of center would put the ball on the target 8 inches to the right of the center of the target at 200 yards, 24 inches at 600 yards, and 40 inches at 1,000 yards. Do not forget the fact that the wind allowance on a rear sight should be toward the wind; *the opposite of allowance on a wind-gauge on the muzzle.*

It would seem at first thought that at long ranges much more allowance should be made than at mid ranges. While this is slightly true, the error lies in the exaggeration. The farther you are from the target the greater the deviation would be for a given allowance on a still day; the increased distance for the ball to cover gives more opportunity for the wind to act on it, so, one balances the other to a great extent. There is but one military arm known to the writer where the sliding bar, between the uprights, does not allow windage enough for a half gale. For a gale make your allowance less, aiming at the next target to hit your own.

The point to be aimed at on the target will have to be varied for fluctuations in wind in view of the fact that the aim must be taken over lines 1-32 of an inch apart. The complication attendant upon trying to divide distance between lines on the rear sight is too great, principally from the fact that the focus of the eye must be changed to enable it to be done. As far as possible let the eye observe the sights uniformly and make your allowances on the face of the target—a wider field for judgment of distance and requiring but one effort of the eye, viz.: to see. Divide the distance from right to left as best you can for fluctuations in wind.

The author recommends that the sights be smoked a dead black and kept so throughout the shooting.

When so much is conquered, apply yourself carefully to the other pages of this book.

In reloading ammunition for a military rifle, if your firing pin is of such make as to be safe, place the shell in the chamber and close the breech-block; having gotten it in once, if you mark the shell, you will have no trouble, on the field, in putting it in again. Pour your powder in slowly from the muzzle; this packs it properly. Put in a thin but tough wad (the best are made out of lithographic press paper), send it home sure. Put in a disc of lubricant (to be had at all gun houses). Put in the bullet, and when it is home, put your weight on the rod three times.

This way of making cartridges is excellent; it will be better than if machine made, because the powder is packed, not crushed. They will keep nicely, the lubricant hermetically sealing them.

Capt. W. H. JACKSON, Boston, Mass.

Captain American Team of 1878. Winner of the Long Range Tournament, 1879.
True Off-Hand Position.

Capt. Jackson has made the following records in this position, Walnut Hill Range, December 6th, 1879, 200 yards:

Ten Shots, - 5 5 5 5 5 5 5 5 5 4 - - -	Total, 49	out of 50.
Fifteen Shots, 5 5 5 5 5 5 5 5 4 5 5 5 5 5 - -	" 74	" 75.
Twenty Shots, 5 5 5 5 5 5 5 5 5 4 5 5 5 5 5 4 4 5 5 5	" 97	" 100.

With a *Military* rifle (regulation open sights), the Captain has made 48 out of 50 twice, and 47 out of 50 several times.

40 CHESTNUT STREET,
BOSTON, Feb. 24, 1880.

CAPTAIN E. A. PERRY.

MY DEAR CAPTAIN:

To answer your desire "that I will state my reasons for advocating true OFF-HAND position, and to describe the position for the benefit of others," I will first say that I began shooting by resting the arm against the body, balancing the rifle upon the ends of my fingers, and had to learn over again when I took up off-hand shooting.

The position is simple. Seize the piece between the thumb and forefinger, bent (in fact all the fingers tightly closed, to stiffen the muscles of the forearm) about six inches in front of the trigger guard, hand well under the piece; grasp the small of the stock firmly with the right hand, and raise the piece to the shoulder; do not bend the knees or back, nor couch down in an awkward position; stand erect, and bring the rifle up; feel perfectly easy; carry the left elbow well under the piece, raise the right elbow level with the shoulder, drop the head slightly forward, resting the cheek upon the stock. When the aim is perfect, do not pull with a jerk, but press the trigger firmly, noticing where the gun is pointing at the instant of discharge, and see if the marker verifies it. Have the hole in the peep cup large, or the target will be indistinct. Mark the shells, and put them in the same side up and they will give better service.

We shoot for pleasure and health. Let us cultivate that style of holding the rifle which gives the greatest freedom and ease; and as the school of the soldier is to make the man erect and graceful, so let us cultivate that grace of position in our noble sport of rifle shooting. I made, in a match at Walnut Hill, on the 6th of December, 1879, in ten consecutive shots, 49; in fifteen consecutive shots, 74; in twenty consecutive shots, 97.

I am, respectfully,

W. H. JACKSON.

PAGE.	SUMMARY.					WIND.	
	OCCASION.	DATE.	TIME.	WEATHER.	Light.	Direction.	FOR

Thermometer.	Barometer.	Hygrometer.	SUMMARY.				Score.	ELEVATIONS.			
			Bullet.	Powder.	Rifle.	Sight.		1,100	800	900	1,000

CREEDMOOR RANGE HOTEL.

NORTH SIDE OF R. R. DEPOT.

JOHN KLEIN,
Proprietor.

With a view to affording ample accommodations to all who visit Creedmoor Range, Mr KLEIN respectfully begs to announce to his patrons and friends, that he has recently erected the handsome and commodious hotel on the north Side of the Railroad Depot, within three minutes walk of the Rifle Range and he invites all to come and inspect the premises. It will be his constant aim to satisfactorily cater to the wants of his guests, and so merit a continuance of the patronage so generously bestowed upon him in the past.

REFRESHMENTS OF ALL KINDS, ALES, WINES, LIQUORS AND CIGARS, KEPT CONSTANTLY ON HAND.

The Cuisine of the Hotel is under the very best Management.

Lunches, Dinners and Suppers excellently prepared and promptly served.

UNEXCELLED ACCOMMODATIONS FOR PRIVATE PARTIES.

Board by the Day, Week or Month.

CREEDMOOR HOTEL.

DOSCHER & JOOST,

Successors to Capt. L. G. T. BRUER,

Have enlarged their Hotel, and offer to their Patrons, Accommodations in

TWO DEPARTMENTS.

IN THE LARGE NEW DINING ROOM,

All Refreshments will be served; as also,

WINES, ALES, LAGER, LIQUORS, SEGARS, &c.

The old place formerly occupied by Capt. Bruer, will be retained as strictly a

TEMPERANCE LUNCH ROOM.

LOCKERS TO RENT AS BEFORE.

A LARGE HALL

Has been put over the old place, and a **FINE BALCONY,** where the Shooting can be seen.

Century Hotel.

Has been thoroughly renovated, and furnished throughout with *New Furniture*, for the accommodation of those who wish to remain over at the Range, and for **FAMILIES TO BOARD** at reasonable rates.

CAPT. BRUER WILL HAVE CHARGE OF THE LOCKERS.

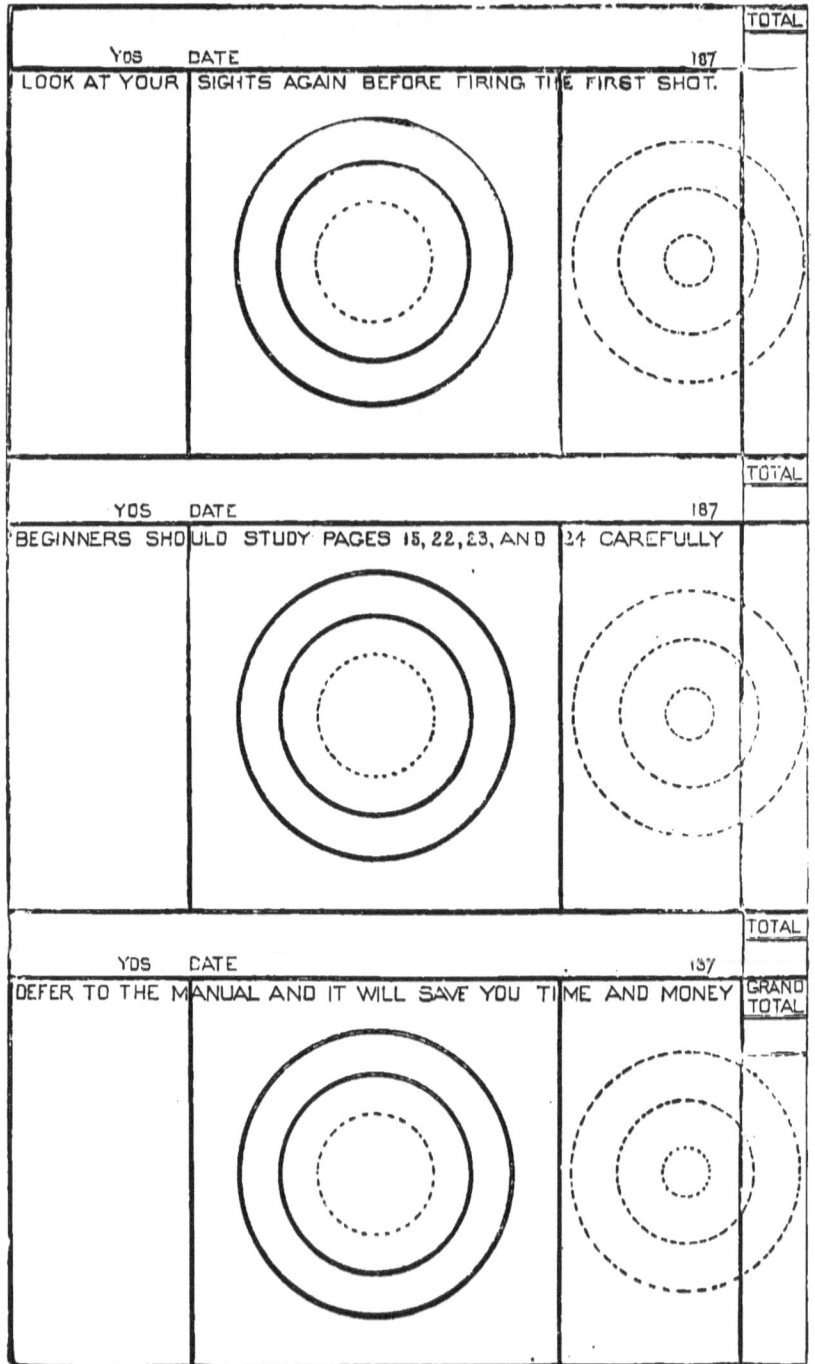

	2	3	4	5	6	7	8	9	10	11	12	13	14	15

SIGHT   POWDER   BULLET

	2	3	4	5	6	7	8	9	10	11	12	13	14	15

SIGHT   POWDER   BULLET

	2	3	4	5	6	7	8	9	10	11	12	13	14	15

SIGHT   POWDER   BULLET

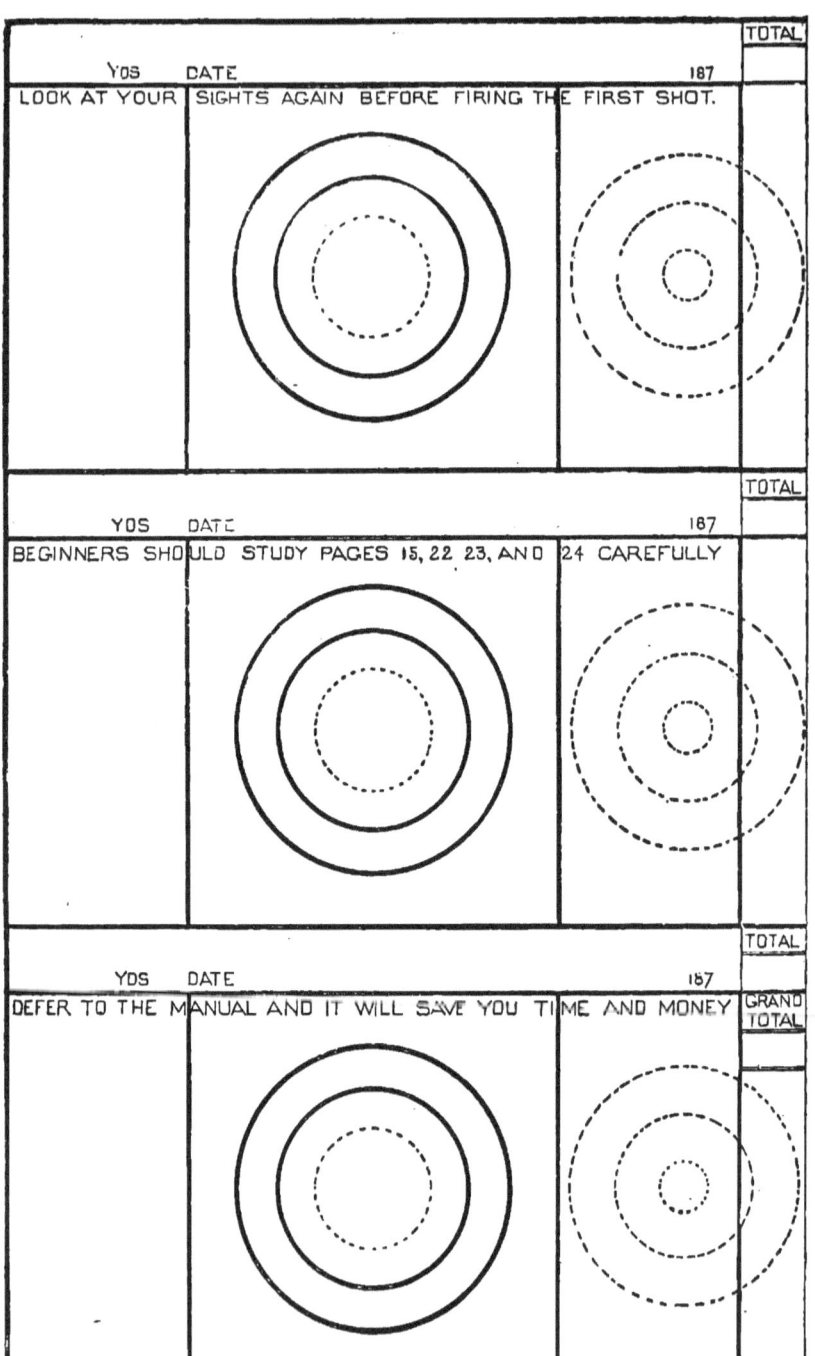

| 5 | 6 | 7 | 8 | 9 | 10 | 11 | 12 | 13 | 14 |

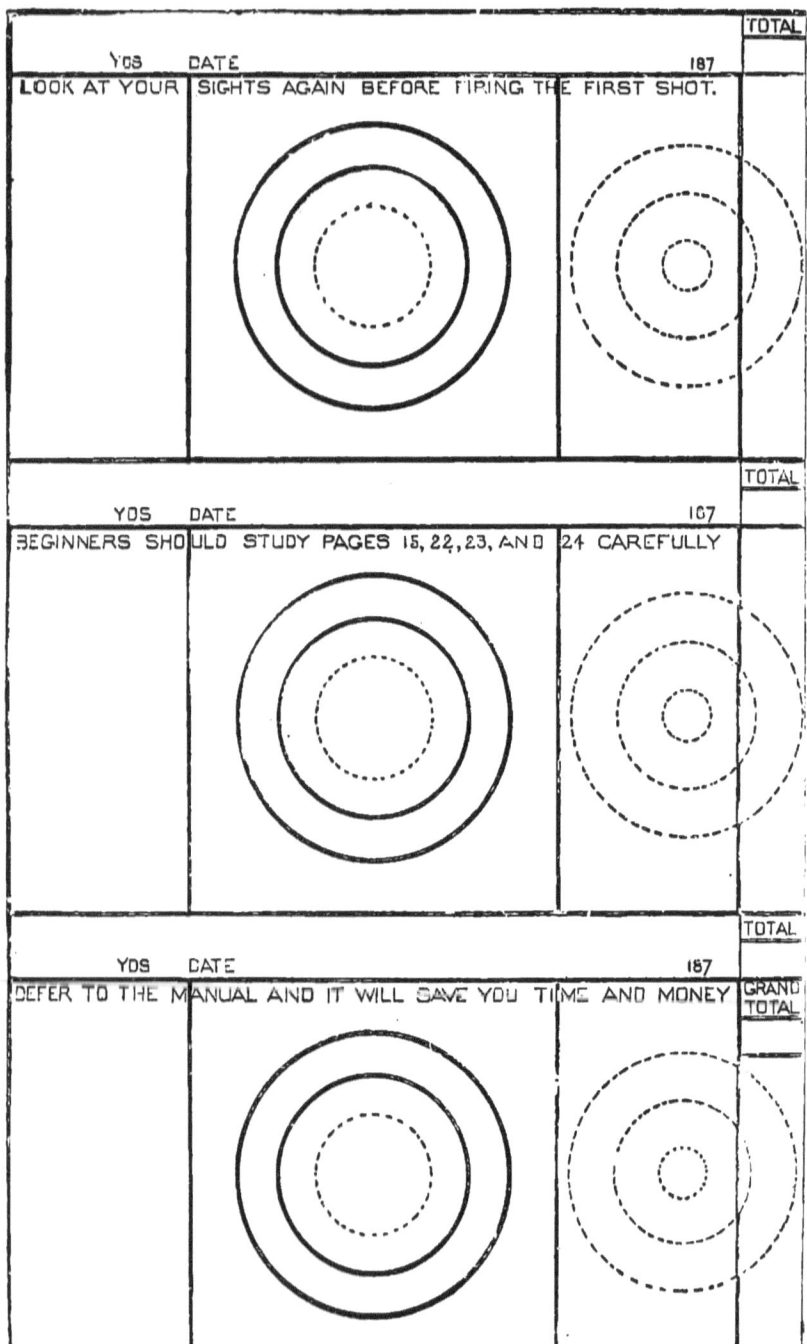

No OF SHOT	1	2	3	4	5	6	7	8	9	10	11	12	13	14	15
SCORE															
ELEVATION															
WIND GAUGE															
" DIRECTION															
WEATHER															
LIGHT															
THERMO DRY															
METER WET															
BAROMETER															
RIFLE			SIGHT				POWDER				BULLET				
TIME															
No OF SHOT	1	2	3	4	5	6	7	8	9	10	11	12	13	14	15
SCORE															
ELEVATION															
WIND GAUGE															
" DIRECTION															
WEATHER															
LIGHT															
THERMO DRY															
METER WET															
BAROMETER															
RIFLE			SIGHT				POWDER				BULLET				
TIME															
No OF SHOT	1	2	3	4	5	6	7	8	9	10	11	12	13	14	15
SCORE															
ELEVATION															
WIND GAUGE															
" DIRECTION															
WEATHER															
LIGHT															
THERMO DRY															
METER WET															
BAROMETER															
RIFLE			SIGHT				POWDER				BULLET				
TIME															

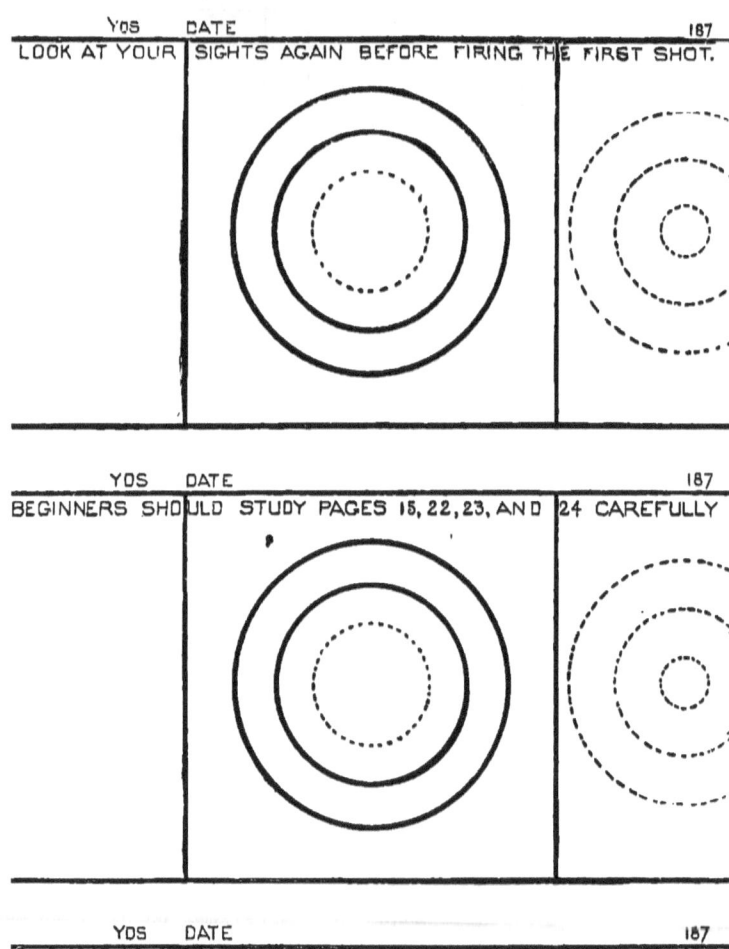

YDS DATE   187
LOOK AT YOUR SIGHTS AGAIN BEFORE FIRING THE FIRST SHOT.

YDS DATE   187
BEGINNERS SHOULD STUDY PAGES 15, 22, 23, AND 24 CAREFULLY

YDS DATE   187
DEFER TO THE MANUAL AND IT WILL SAVE YOU TIME AND MONEY

N° OF SHOT	1	2	3	4	5	6	7	8	9	10	11	12	13	14	15
SCORE															
ELEVATION															
WIND GAUGE															
" DIRECTION															
WEATHER															
LIGHT															
THERMO- DRY															
METER WET															
BAROMETER															
RIFLE			SIGHT				POWDER				BULLET				
TIME															

N° OF SHOT	1	2	3	4	5	6	7	8	9	10	11	12	13	14	15
SCORE															
ELEVATION															
WIND GAUGE															
" DIRECTION															
WEATHER															
LIGHT															
THERMO- DRY															
METER WET															
BAROMETER															
RIFLE			SIGHT				POWDER				BULLET				
TIME															

N° OF SHOT	1	2	3	4	5	6	7	8	9	10	11	12	13	14	15
SCORE															
ELEVATION															
WIND GAUGE															
" DIRECTION															
WEATHER															
LIGHT															
THERMO- DRY															
METER WET															
BAROMETER															
RIFLE			SIGHT				POWDER				BULLET				
TIME															

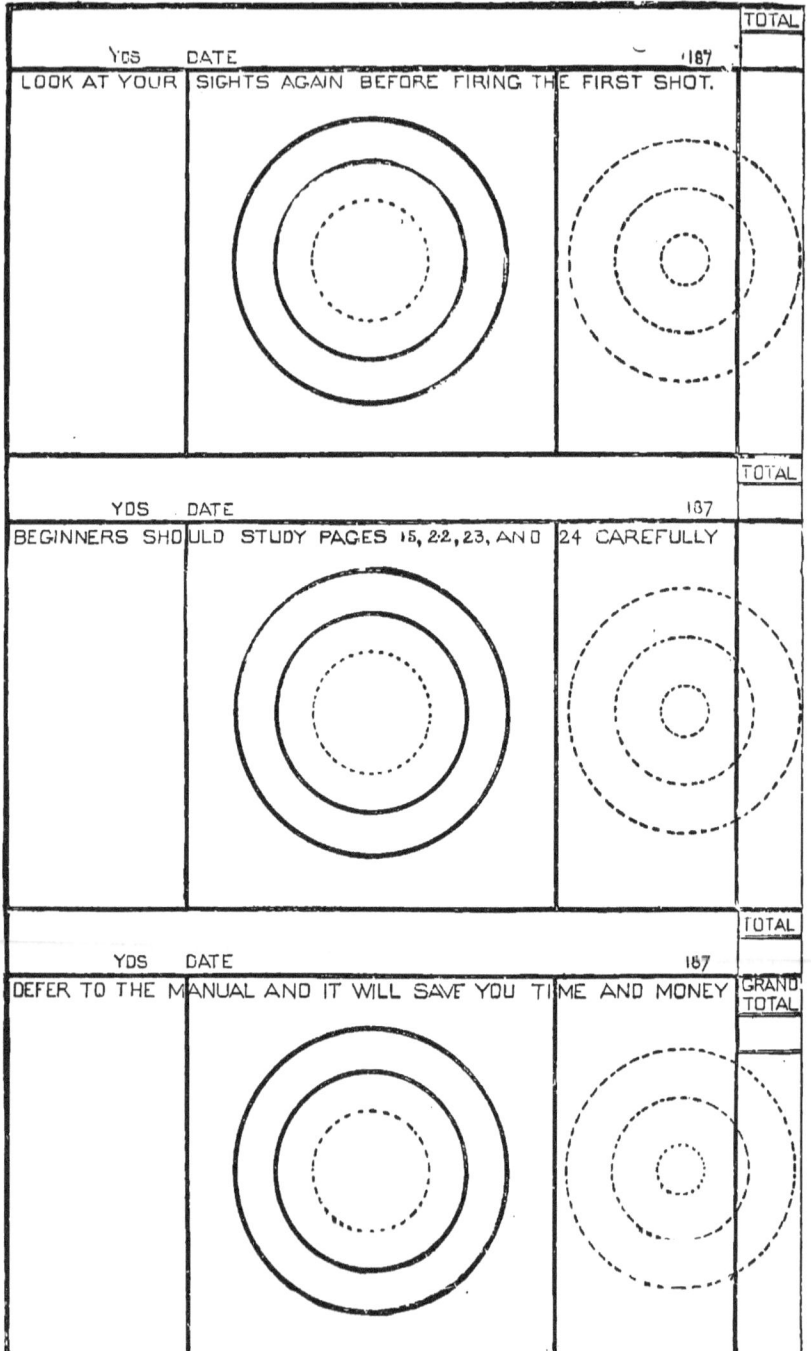

7	8	9	10	11	12	1

POWDER   BULLET

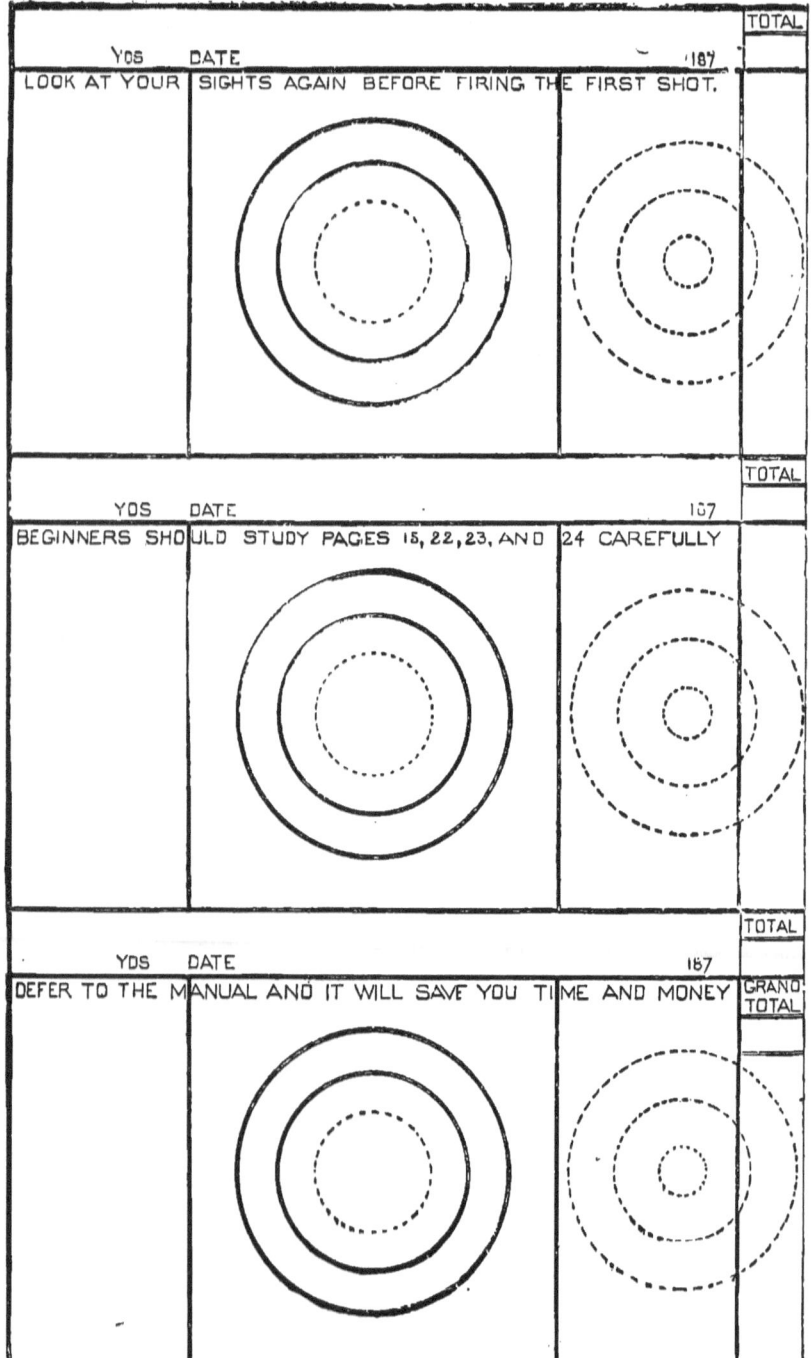

101

3	4	5	6	7	8	9	10	11	12	1

SIGHT   POWDER   BULLET

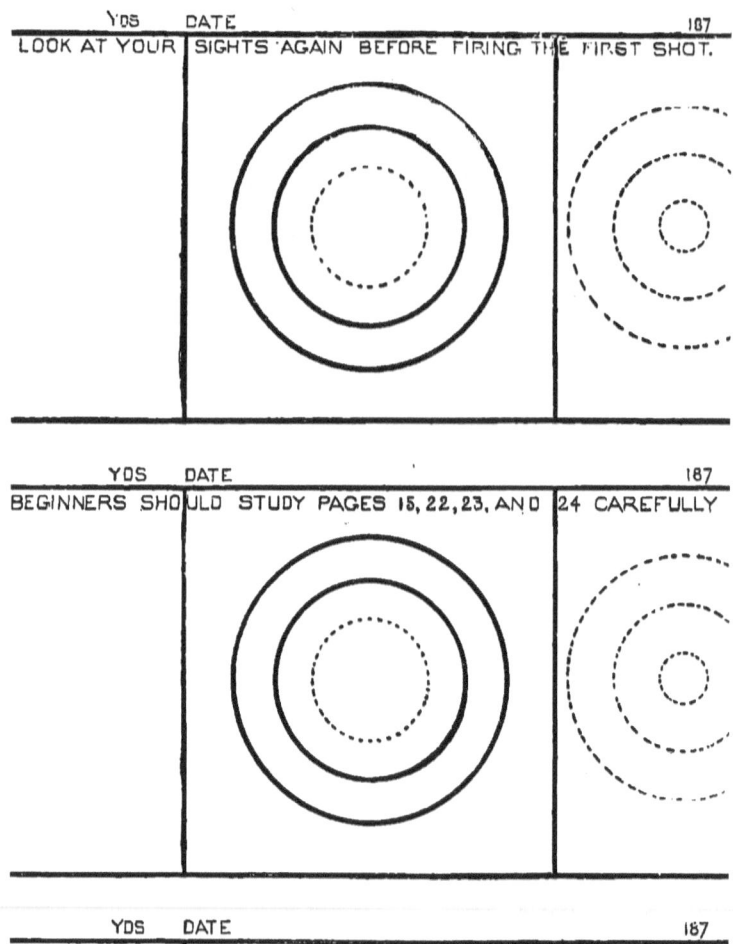

7	8	9	10	11	12	1
		.				
				,		
			.			

POWDER   BULLET

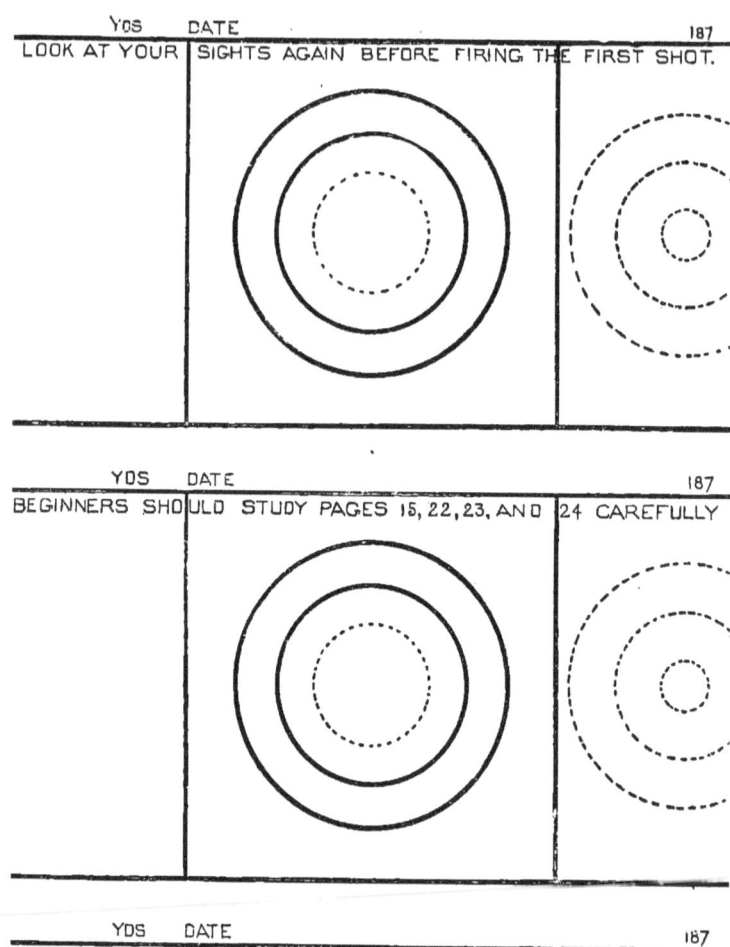

	6	7	8	9	10	11	12	13

POWDER   BULLET

	YDS	DATE	187	TOTAL

LOOK AT YOUR SIGHTS AGAIN BEFORE FIRING THE FIRST SHOT.

	YDS	DATE	187	TOTAL

BEGINNERS SHOULD STUDY PAGES 15, 22, 23, AND 24 CAREFULLY

	YDS	DATE	187	TOTAL

DEFER TO THE MANUAL AND IT WILL SAVE YOU TIME AND MONEY

GRAND TOTAL

2	3	4	5	6	7	8	9	10	11	12	13	14	15

SIGHT	POWDER	BULLET

2	3	4	5	6	7	8	9	10	11	12	13	14	15

SIGHT	POWDER	BULLET

2	3	4	5	6	7	8	9	10	11	12	13	14	15

SIGHT	POWDER	BULLET

			TOTAL
YDS DATE		187	
LOOK AT YOUR	SIGHTS AGAIN BEFORE FIRING THE FIRST SHOT.		

			TOTAL
YDS DATE		187	
BEGINNERS SHOULD STUDY PAGES 15, 22 23, AND		24 CAREFULLY	

			TOTAL
YDS DATE		187	GRAND TOTAL
DEFER TO THE MANUAL AND IT WILL SAVE YOU TIME AND MONEY			

	7	8	9	10	11	12	13

POWDER　　　　BULLET

		TOTAL
YDS DATE	187	
LOOK AT YOUR	SIGHTS AGAIN BEFORE FIRING THE FIRST SHOT.	

		TOTAL
YDS DATE	187	
BEGINNERS SHOULD STUDY PAGES 15, 22 23, AND	24 CAREFULLY	

		TOTAL
YDS DATE	187	GRAND TOTAL
DEFER TO THE MANUAL AND IT WILL SAVE YOU TIME AND MONEY		

111

6	7	8	9	10	11	12	13

POWDER   BULLET

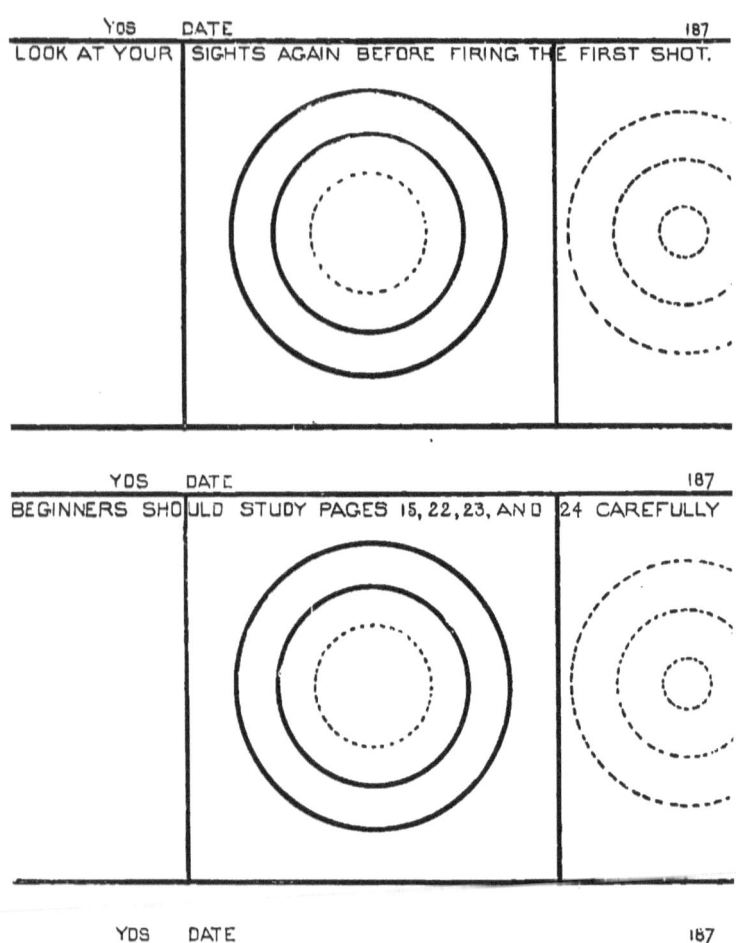

113

3	4	5	6	7	8	9	10	11	12	13
		.								

SIGHT   POWDER   BULLET

114

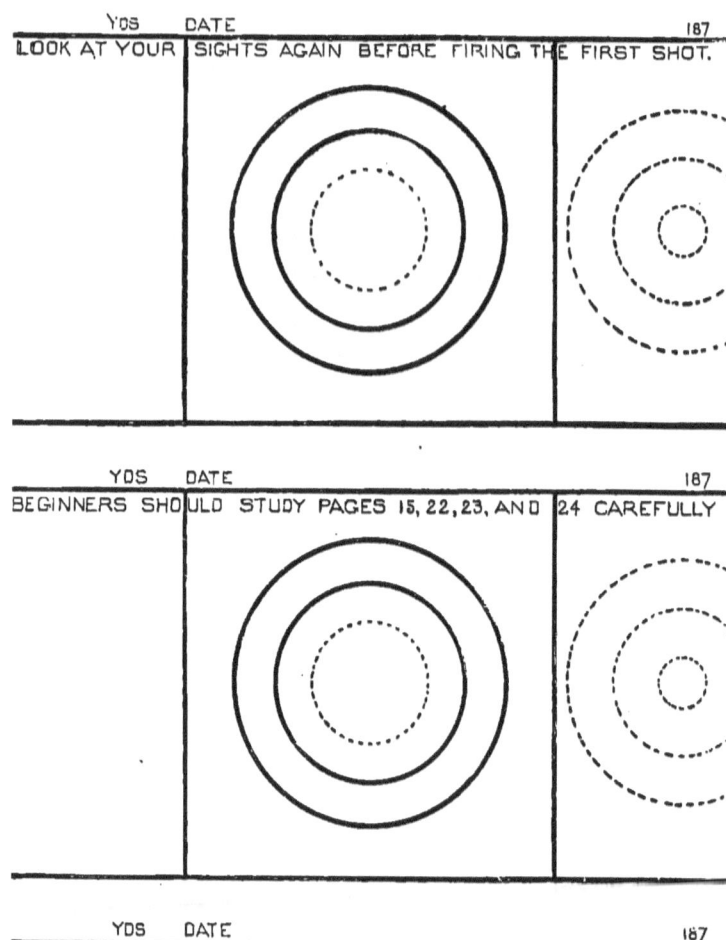

	5	6	7	8	9	10	11	12	13	14
		·								

POWDER   BULLET

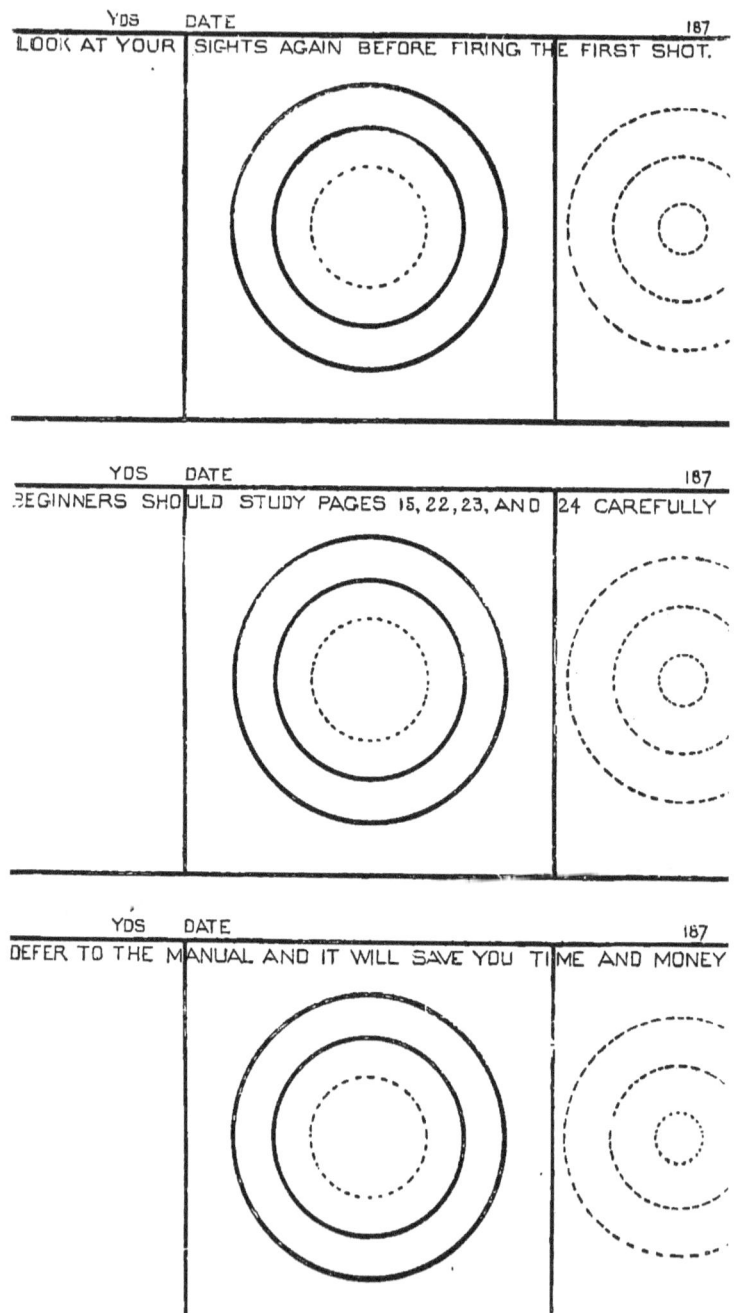

YDS   DATE   187
LOOK AT YOUR SIGHTS AGAIN BEFORE FIRING THE FIRST SHOT.

YDS   DATE   187
BEGINNERS SHOULD STUDY PAGES 15, 22, 23, AND 24 CAREFULLY

YDS   DATE   187
DEFER TO THE MANUAL AND IT WILL SAVE YOU TIME AND MONEY

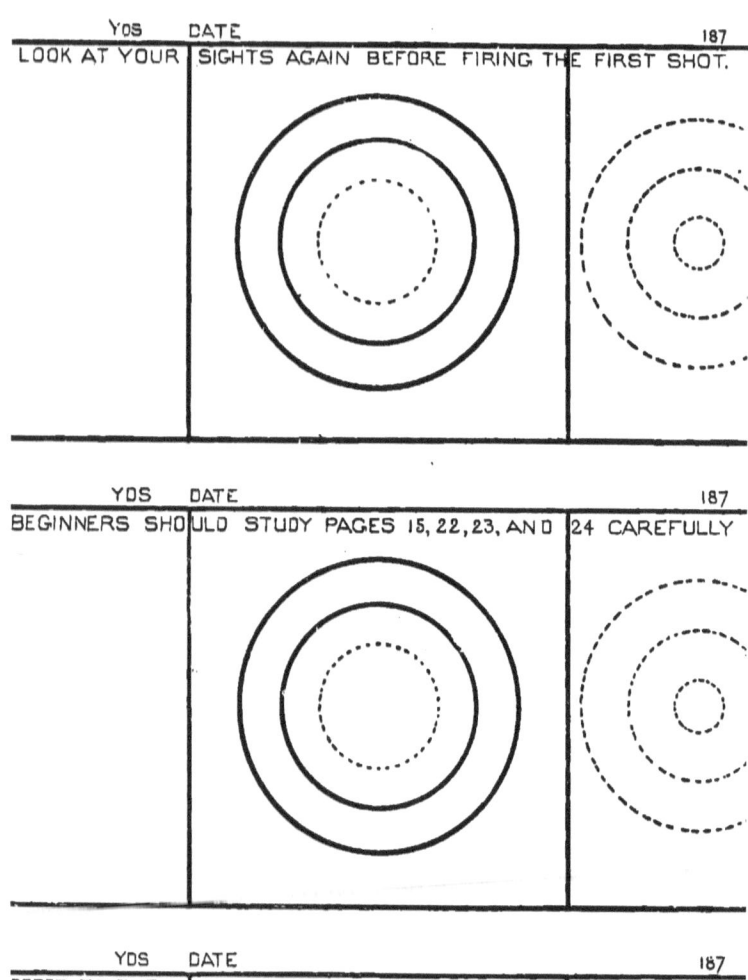

| YDS | DATE | | 187 |

LOOK AT YOUR SIGHTS AGAIN BEFORE FIRING THE FIRST SHOT.

| YDS | DATE | | 187 |

BEGINNERS SHOULD STUDY PAGES 15, 22, 23, AND 24 CAREFULLY

| YDS | DATE | | 187 |

DEFER TO THE MANUAL AND IT WILL SAVE YOU TIME AND MONEY

	POWDER					BULLET			
5	6	7	8	9	10	11	12	13	14

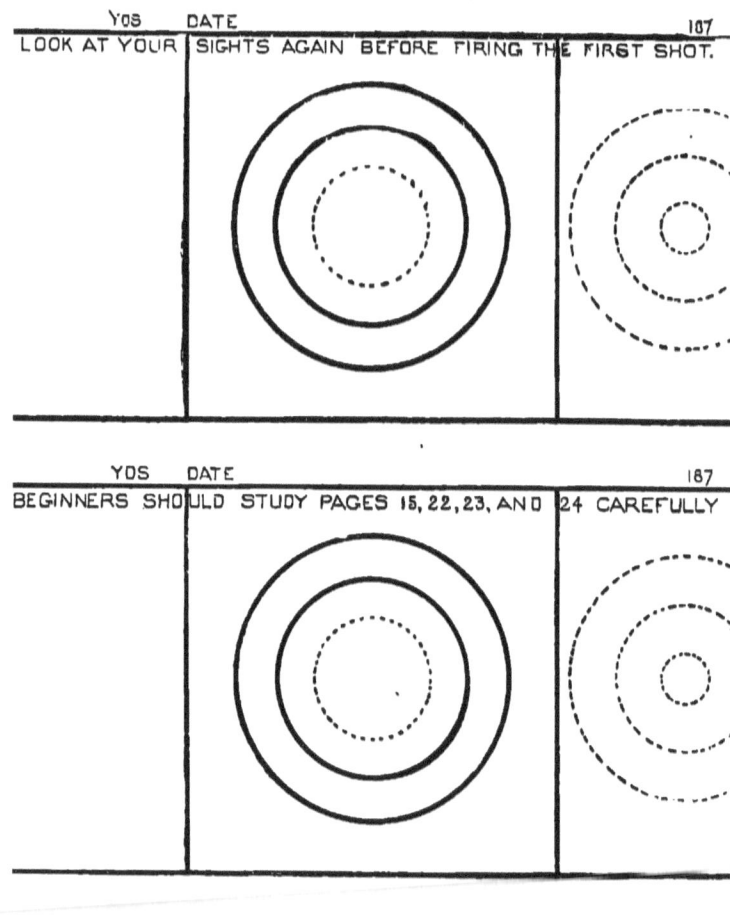

No OF SHOT	1	2	3	4	5	6	7	8	9	10	11	12	13	14	15
SCORE															
ELEVATION															
WIND GAUGE															
" DIRECTION															
WEATHER															
LIGHT															
THERMO DRY															
METER WET															
BAROMETER															
RIFLE		SIGHT			POWDER				BULLET						
TIME															

No OF SHOT	1	2	3	4	5	6	7	8	9	10	11	12	13	14	15
SCORE															
ELEVATION															
WIND GAUGE															
" DIRECTION															
WEATHER															
LIGHT															
THERMO DRY															
METER WET															
BAROMETER															
RIFLE		SIGHT			POWDER				BULLET						
TIME															

No OF SHOT	1	2	3	4	5	6	7	8	9	10	11	12	13	14	15
SCORE															
ELEVATION															
WIND GAUGE															
" DIRECTION															
WEATHER															
LIGHT															
THERMO DRY															
METER WET															
BAROMETER															
RIFLE		SIGHT			POWDER				BULLET						
TIME															

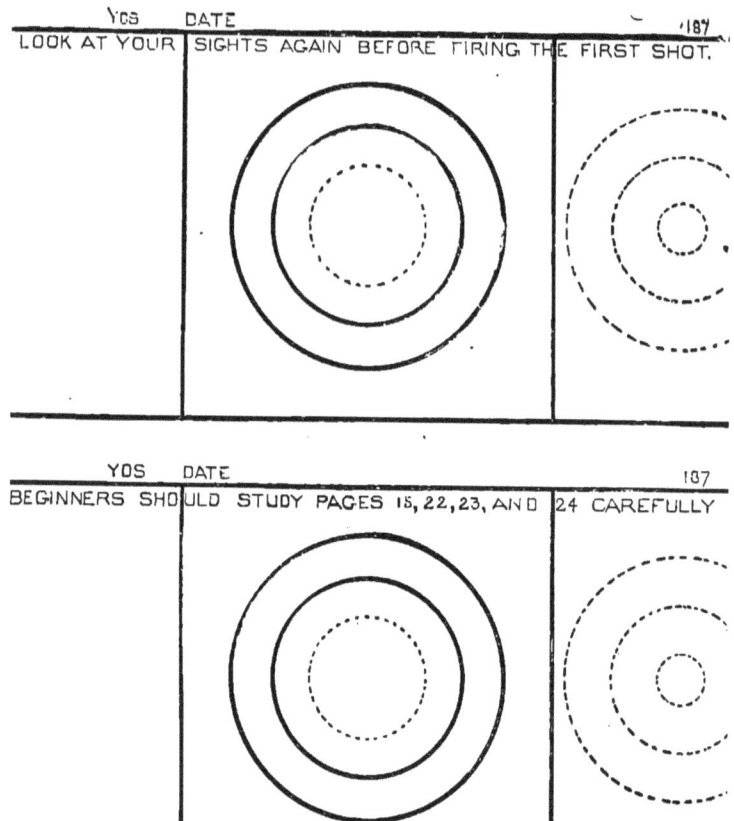

No OF SHOT	1	2	3	4	5	6	7	8	9	10	11	12	13	14	15
SCORE															
ELEVATION															
WIND GAUGE															
" DIRECTION															
WEATHER															
LIGHT															
THERMO DRY															
METER WET															
BAROMETER															
RIFLE			SIGHT				POWDER				BULLET				
TIME															
No OF SHOT	1	2	3	4	5	6	7	8	9	10	11	12	13	14	15
SCORE															
ELEVATION															
WIND GAUGE															
" DIRECTION															
WEATHER															
LIGHT															
THERMO DRY															
METER WET															
BAROMETER															
RIFLE			SIGHT				POWDER				BULLET				
TIME															
No OF SHOT	1	2	3	4	5	6	7	8	9	10	11	12	13	14	15
SCORE															
ELEVATION															
WIND GAUGE															
" DIRECTION															
WEATHER															
LIGHT															
THERMO DRY															
METER WET															
BAROMETER															
RIFLE			SIGHT				POWDER				BULLET				
TIME															

		TOTAL
YDS DATE 187		
LOOK AT YOUR SIGHTS AGAIN BEFORE FIRING THE FIRST SHOT.		
		TOTAL
YDS DATE 187		
BEGINNERS SHOULD STUDY PAGES 15, 22, 23, AND 24 CAREFULLY		
		TOTAL
YDS DATE 187		
DEFER TO THE MANUAL AND IT WILL SAVE YOU TIME AND MONEY		GRAND TOTAL

2	3	4	5	6	7	8	9	10	11	12	13	14	15

SIGHT POWDER BULLET

2	3	4	5	6	7	8	9	10	11	12	13	14	15

SIGHT POWDER BULLET

2	3	4	5	6	7	8	9	10	11	12	13	14	15

SIGHT POWDER BULLET

| YDS | DATE | 187 | TOTAL |

LOOK AT YOUR SIGHTS AGAIN BEFORE FIRING THE FIRST SHOT.

| YDS | DATE | 187 | TOTAL |

BEGINNERS SHOULD STUDY PAGES 15, 22, 23, AND 24 CAREFULLY

| YDS | DATE | 187 | TOTAL |

DEFER TO THE MANUAL AND IT WILL SAVE YOU TIME AND MONEY

GRAND TOTAL

	POWDER					BULLET			
5	6	7	8	9	10	11	12	13	14

			TOTAL
YDS DATE 187			
LOOK AT YOUR	SIGHTS AGAIN BEFORE FIRING THE FIRST SHOT.		

			TOTAL
YDS DATE 187			
BEGINNERS SHOULD STUDY PAGES 15, 22, 23, AND		24 CAREFULLY	

			TOTAL
YDS DATE 187			
DEFER TO THE MANUAL AND IT WILL SAVE YOU TIME AND MONEY			GRAND TOTAL

	2	3	4	5	6	7	8	9	10	11	12	13

SIGHT   POWDER   BULLET

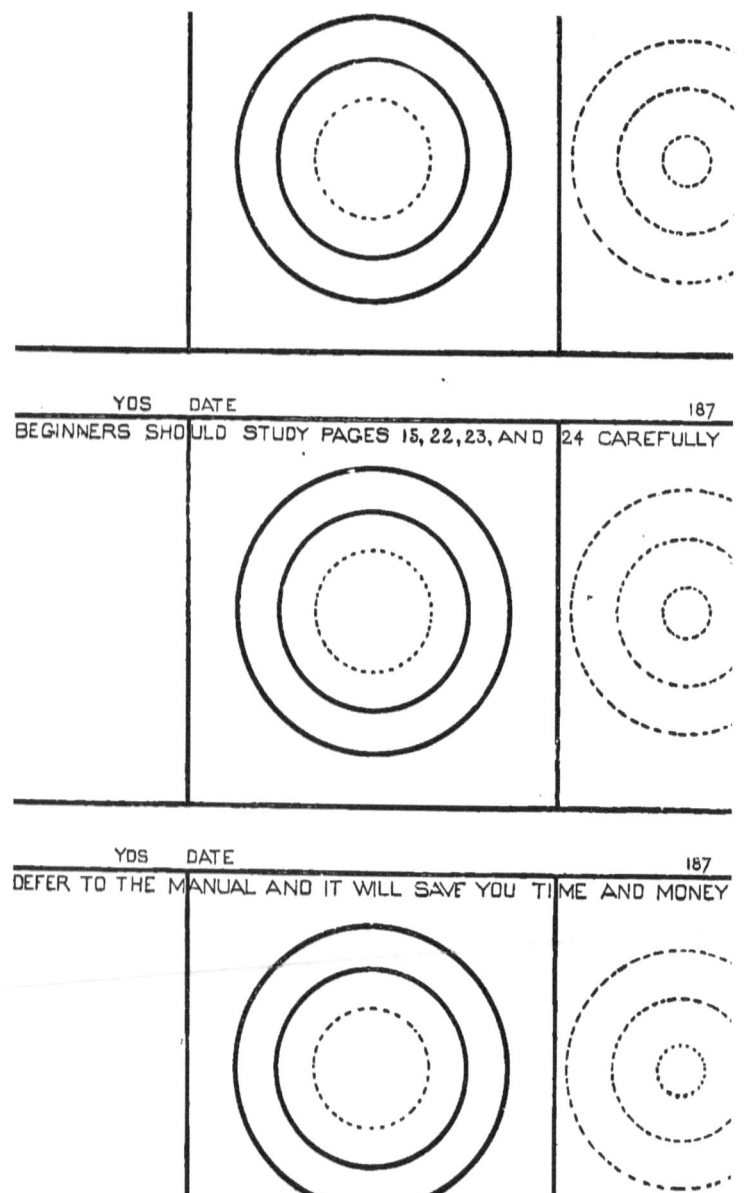

YDS DATE 187
BEGINNERS SHOULD STUDY PAGES 15, 22, 23, AND 24 CAREFULLY

YDS DATE 187
DEFER TO THE MANUAL AND IT WILL SAVE YOU TIME AND MONEY

	6	7	8	9	10	11	12	13

POWDER   BULLET

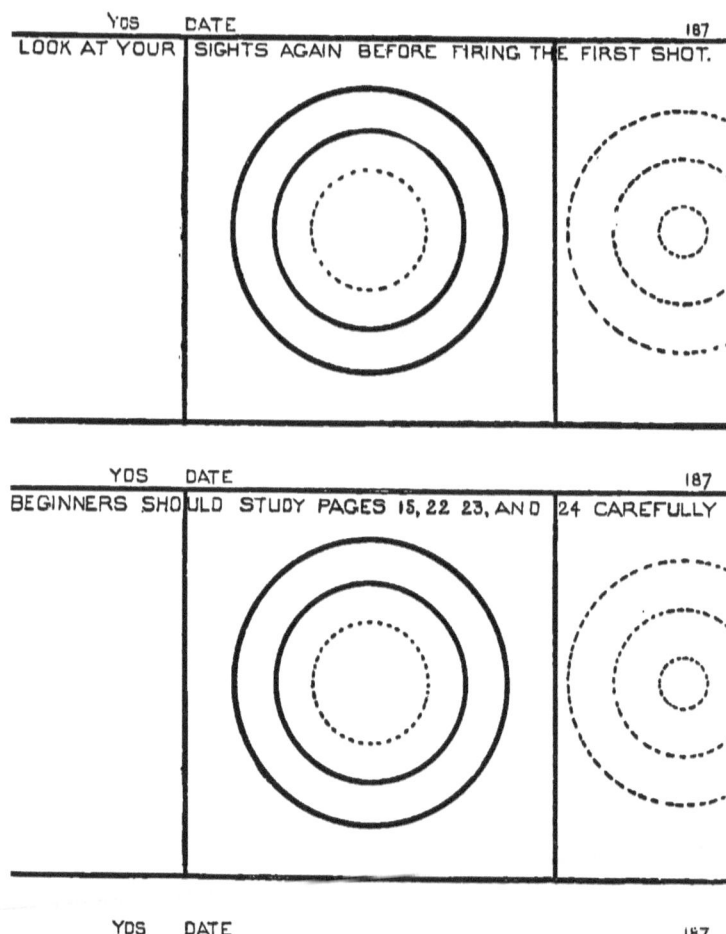

2	3	4	5	6	7	8	9	10	11	12	13	14	15

SIGHT　　POWDER　　BULLET

2	3	4	5	6	7	8	9	10	11	12	13	14	15

SIGHT　　POWDER　　BULLET

2	3	4	5	6	7	8	9	10	11	12	13	14	15

SIGHT　　POWDER　　BULLET

	YDS	DATE			TOTAL
				187	
LOOK AT YOUR	SIGHTS AGAIN BEFORE FIRING THE FIRST SHOT.				

	YDS	DATE			TOTAL
				187	
BEGINNERS SHOULD STUDY PAGES 15, 22 23, AND 24 CAREFULLY					

	YDS	DATE			TOTAL
				187	GRAND TOTAL
DEFER TO THE MANUAL AND IT WILL SAVE YOU TIME AND MONEY					

SIGHT			POWDER				BULLET		
3	4	5	6	7	8	9	10	11	12	13

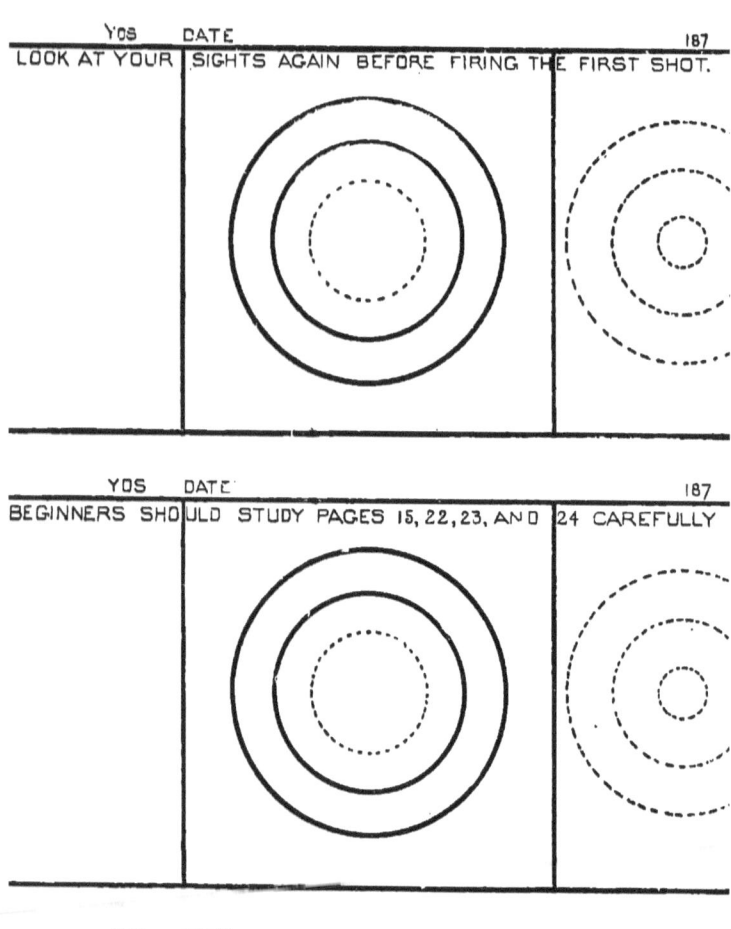

SIGHT			POWDER				BULLET			
3	4	5	6	7	8	9	10	11	12	13	14

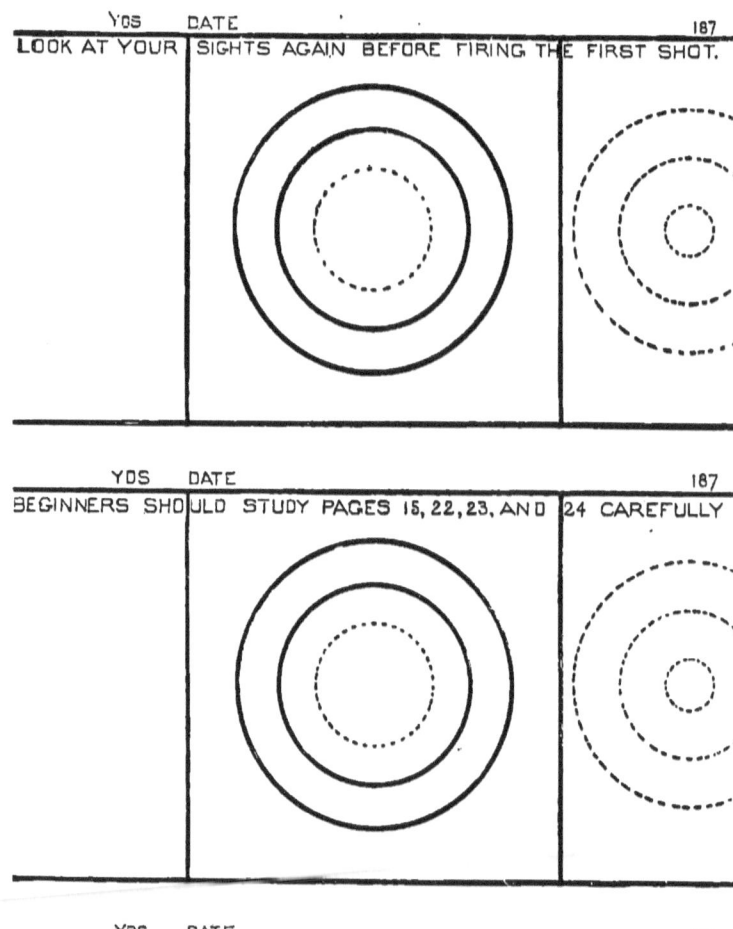

YDS   DATE   187
LOOK AT YOUR SIGHTS AGAIN BEFORE FIRING THE FIRST SHOT.

YDS   DATE   187
BEGINNERS SHOULD STUDY PAGES 15, 22, 23, AND 24 CAREFULLY

YDS   DATE   187
DEFER TO THE MANUAL AND IT WILL SAVE YOU TIME AND MONEY

	2	3	4	5	6	7	8	9	10	11	12	13	14	15

SIGHT　　　　POWDER　　　　BULLET

	2	3	4	5	6	7	8	9	10	11	12	13	14	15

SIGHT　　　　POWDER　　　　BULLET

	2	3	4	5	6	7	8	9	10	11	12	13	14	15

SIGHT　　　　POWDER　　　　BULLET

ORANGE POWDER.

Laflin & Rand Powder Co.,

26 Murray Street, New York City.

The ORANGE MILLS, celebrated for seventy years, still find favor with Sportsmen.

ORANGE POWDER is recommended and used by CAPT. A. H. BOGARDUS, the "Champion Wing Shot of the World."

CREEDMOOR BRAND.

The brand above mentioned possesses, with sufficient density, great strength and cleanliness, and it has commended itself to the most competent judges.

RIFLE PRACTICE MADE EASY.

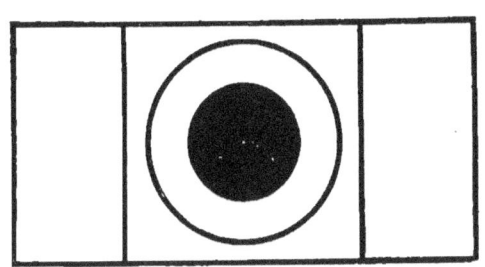

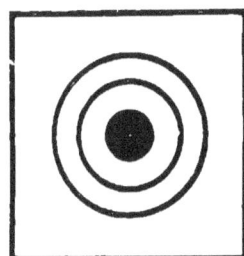 ## DENNISON'S TARGETS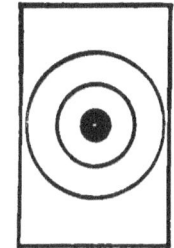

For all Ranges, from 25 to 1000 Yards.

TARGET PASTERS AND SCORE CARDS,

ALSO,

TARGETS AND PADS,

FOR TESTING THE PATTERN AND PENETRATION OF SHOT GUNS.

SOLD BY DEALERS IN SPORTING GOODS.

On receipt of TEN CENTS, we will send by mail a

ONE HUNDRED YARD TARGET,

with Circular containing MAJOR HENRY FULTON'S RULES FOR PRIVATE PRACTICE.

DENNISON & CO.,
198 BROADWAY, NEW YORK.

www.ingramcontent.com/pod-product-compliance
Lightning Source LLC
Chambersburg PA
CBHW022130160426
43197CB00009B/1223